Jennifer,

May your glass
be filled with
nothing but the
very best!

xo Sonia

five
wine scoring system

TONIA MCARTHUR

Published by **Tonia McArthur Enterprises**
toniamcarthur.com
⊙ tonia.mcarthur

First Hardcover Edition May 2022

ISBN 978-1-7781572-0-2

Artwork by Nessa Lovell
Cover and Interior Design by Karolina Wudniak
Editing by Ursula Acton
Illustrations by Jasmine Waller

To my husband and our two sweet daughters. Thank you for teaching me the importance of living in my joy. You are my moon and stars.

Table of Contents

wine:	out-of-five	66
wine:	out-of-five	68
wine:	out-of-five	70
wine:	out-of-five	72
wine:	out-of-five	74
wine:	out-of-five	76
wine:	out-of-five	78
wine:	out-of-five	80
wine:	out-of-five	82
wine:	out-of-five	84
wine:	out-of-five	86
wine:	out-of-five	88
wine:	out-of-five	90
wine:	out-of-five	92
wine:	out-of-five	94
wine:	out-of-five	96
wine:	out-of-five	98
wine:	out-of-five	100
wine:	out-of-five	102
wine:	out-of-five	104
wine:	out-of-five	106
wine:	out-of-five	108
wine:	out-of-five	110
wine:	out-of-five	112
wine:	out-of-five	114

wine:	out-of-five	116
wine:	out-of-five	118
wine:	out-of-five	120
wine:	out-of-five	122
wine:	out-of-five	124
wine:	out-of-five	126
wine:	out-of-five	128
wine:	out-of-five	130
wine:	out-of-five	132
wine:	out-of-five	134
wine:	out-of-five	136
wine:	out-of-five	138
wine:	out-of-five	140
wine:	out-of-five	142
wine:	out-of-five	144
wine:	out-of-five	146
wine:	out-of-five	148
wine:	out-of-five	150
wine:	out-of-five	152
wine:	out-of-five	154
wine:	out-of-five	156
wine:	out-of-five	158
wine:	out-of-five	160
wine:	out-of-five	162
wine:	out-of-five	164

introduction

Have you purchased a bottle of wine just because it was on sale?

Have you ever decided to buy a bottle of wine because of its label?

Have you ever been to a winery for a tasting and nodded your head in agreement even though you didn't really understand what their wine descriptions meant?

Do you end up buying wines you don't really like, wishing you understood how to choose the ones you do?

Maybe you love wine and you're familiar with a lot of varietals but you're looking to broaden your horizons and sharpen your wine tasting skills.

High Five Wine Scoring System and **High Five Wine Academy** offer the instruction and practice to become the expert of your palate. This idea of knowing our own likes and dislikes helps us communicate in a language that can be kind of tricky to understand. We hear words associated with wine like acidity, complexity and off dry but what do they really mean?

That's what we're here to figure out, because everybody who enjoys drinking wine should drink the wine they enjoy.

I'm here to teach you how to be your own wine critic with a system that is simple, fun and based on your taste. This puts you in the driver's seat,

easing the pressure of having to know what the experts know. Instead, you will learn to identify and express your wine preferences with descriptive language by becoming the expert of your palate. The High Five Wine Scoring System lets you flip the script, bridging the gap between wine drinker and wine expert.

The truth is this system was just a little something I put together for me and my husband to use when we were totally geeking out over a new wine we hadn't tried before. We continued to use and tweak it as we went, finding that scoring our wines was pretty useful and a really fun way to start a date night.

On one of those date nights, in the middle of a tasting together, it hit me! This is something everyone can learn, not just my husband and me. If I could show people how to use this system, this would help to build confidence in purchasing and enjoying good, and even great, wine.

I set out writing the details and all of a sudden this incredible and fun concept started coming to life.

Welcome to the High Five Wine Scoring System!

This system breaks down your score of the wines you try out of a total of five. The outline later in this workbook will help you to recognize and isolate your sensory experience with wine and (ultimately!) food as well. What does it mean when your wine is acidic? What happens to your senses? Those are the kinds of things we focus on here. You will develop your palate and learn wine terminology and have a lot of fun doing it.

Follow the five-point system as it is laid out and practice along with us on our **High Five Wine Academy** calls. Join our wine community!

Interested in learning more? Head to my website:

toniamcarthur.com

It is my hope that as your palate evolves, wine will bring you more joy than ever before.

I'm so glad you're here. I can't wait to meet you in our community

xo

Tonia

about me

I have been studying wine for many years, all starting with my WSET Level 1 back in 2012. I have continued my studies, worked as a server and bartender, spent some time at a small specialty wine boutique, started an in-home wine tasting education business, as well as established and run a wine club for a great winery local to me.

Then I had babies.

While pregnant with my second daughter in 2021, I became so sick that I wasn't sure if we were going to make it. When we pulled through, I knew I had to make some changes to my personal and professional life. There was an element of JOY missing and after a very long year of illness, it was time to start implementing the things necessary to bring that back.

What has always brought me joy is studying wine.

This isn't just drinking delicious Montepulciano or fabulous Viognier for me, although that is certainly how the love affair started. It's about the magic in the origins of the grapes, old-world designation systems, the terroir that affects characteristics, and the history. It's the ever-changing industry that resets each year and the climate that keeps us on our toes from vintage to vintage.

If none of that makes sense to you, that's ok, too. This is the story of how we came to be meeting today - in the form of this little workbook that is near and dear to my heart. We will get to know each other and the world of wine through High Five Wine Academy, so be sure to follow me on instagram and watch the highlights for more information **@tonia.mcarthur**. It doesn't matter if you care to study wine in the same way as I do. It matters even less if you and I like the same wines. What does matter is that I can teach you how to keep a record of the wines you love and, sometimes even more importantly, the wines you don't.

Let's find out what they are and why.

Come on!

high five
wine scoring system

Pro Tip:

I once heard that it was a good idea to date stamp your tastings because wine will continue to change in the bottle over time. Sampling a bottle today and another of the same vintage in, let's say, six months might prove to show differences in characteristics. The other important reason is that palates evolve, especially in the early stages of learning to taste wine, and so this should be considered and celebrated.

Be sure to always date your tastings, my friends.

This will also be really helpful in the future if you decide to cellar wine. And, it's just super nerdy and fun to make note of how a wine can change in any varying time frame. No cellaring hobbies needed to geek out over that!

Are you ready to dive into some of the more technical aspects of wine tasting? It all begins with the scoring itself.

What you are about to discover is exactly what I've included in my own scoring system and what I notice or look for in each of the structural elements. Each one is important in helping to decide the ultimate score the wines receive out of five.

Before we pour our wines and get started, here is the breakdown of the **High Five Wine Scoring System** and why it is fun and fit for anyone - from beginner to expert.

one-out-of-five

If a wine receives a one-out-of-five from you it's because this contender simply isn't a wine you would return to. You wouldn't serve it at a party, enjoy a glass on your own or use it to pair with any of the meals you make. A one-out-of-five indicates that you have carefully analyzed each of the structural elements and discovered imbalance without any redeeming qualities. You just don't see potential for improvement.

"It's a 'no' from me."

There is so much wine out in the world, it would be rare if a wine scoring so low would cross your palate again. And that is ok!

two-out-of-five

There is potential for this wine in some capacity but it will take either a lot of time or a superb pairing to dial it in. Worth the wait or all the trouble? Highly unlikely. A two-out-of-five would mean it piques one or more of your senses too much or in a very contrasting way. Say like vanilla ice cream and dill pickles.

So, if you don't like it, why haven't you just straight away given this wine a one-out-of-five?

Well, you really like vanilla ice cream and you also really like dill pickles, you just wouldn't have them together or at the same time. Interesting but really not a combination you find refreshing or enjoyable. This wouldn't be a wine you would serve to guests or enjoy on its own while relaxing - but it might be a wine you talked about because it was interesting enough.

Drinkable? No.

three-out-of-five

Perhaps this wine isn't chock-full of those flavors you adore in a wine of its varietal(s), but you appreciate the effort. It's a sipper and you'd never say no to a glass if someone offered it to you at a party. You would buy this wine yourself and drink it every now and again.

This is a wine you wouldn't kick out of bed.

A **three-out-of-five** has some of the qualities you love but it just doesn't quite make the mark for best of the best. Something is missing. It is not perfect but overall you're "in like" with this dependable wine.

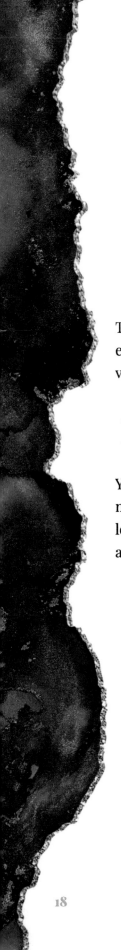

four-out-of-five

This is the perfect example of a wine with the characteristics you would expect. Every last drop has something you love about this specific grape varietal. You could even close your eyes when you have a sip.

Mmm. This is a very good wine.

You want to tell others about it, post it on your social media, have it the next time you make that dinner it's reminding you of. This is a wine you love and you'll buy it over and over. Heck, you'd buy a case of it to stow away in your wine rack.

five-out-of-five

A **HIGH FIVE** is a score reserved for the greats.

These are your Champagnes, your Amarones, your Vernaccias (oh wait, those are some of my high fives). You get it, though.

When a wine receives a **HIGH FIVE**, this means these wines, for you, are unmatched. Think of your absolute most pleasurable wines that typically are reserved for fabulous celebratory occasions or with your masterful meal that guests rave about for weeks. The highest sense of pleasure you have had with a beverage. The glass you pour when you want to indulge. You've had the best day. You've had the worst day. Your guests have finally left and you've saved the good stuff.

What is it?

That's a HIGH FIVE!

If the highest score from a wine critic makes a wine "classic," think about what a "classic" Viognier (or insert one of your favorite wines here) to YOUR palate is like. Not what it should be, but what YOU love the most about a specific wine. **If it's your classic, everything you love — it's a HIGH FIVE.**

aroma & tasting note examples

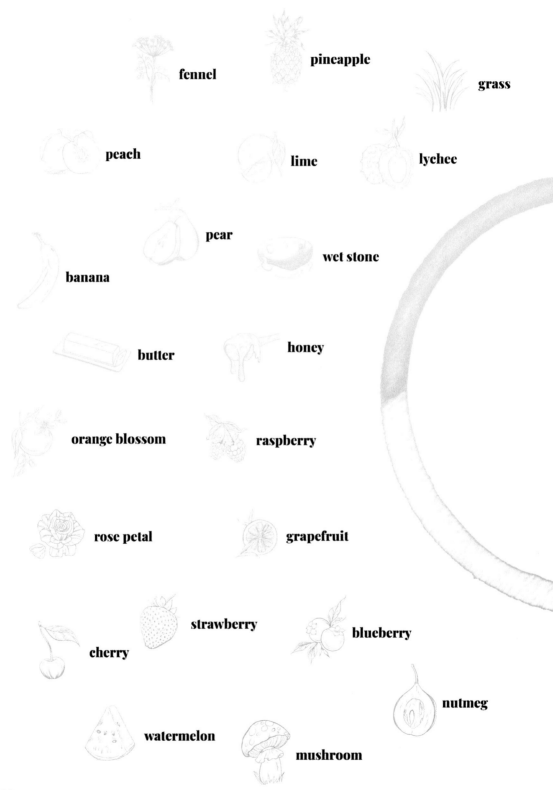

fennel

pineapple

grass

peach

lime

lychee

pear

wet stone

banana

butter

honey

orange blossom

raspberry

rose petal

grapefruit

strawberry

blueberry

cherry

nutmeg

watermelon

mushroom

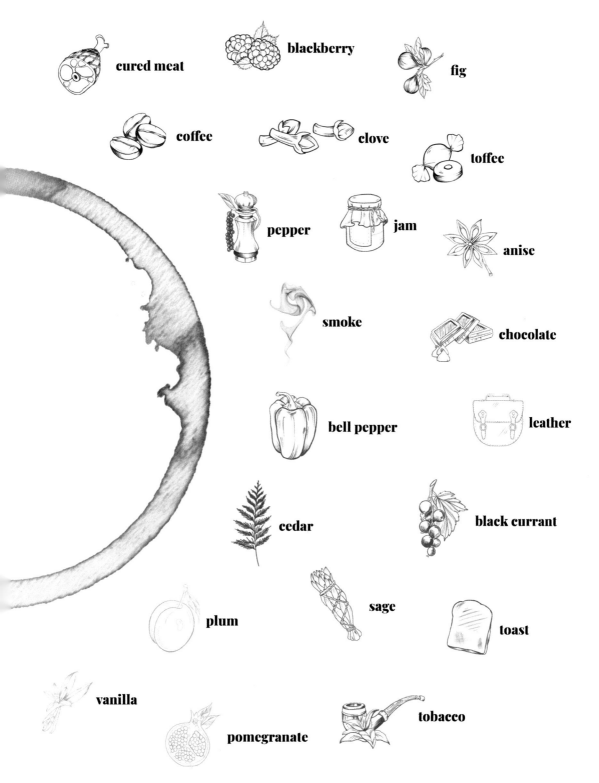

cured meat

blackberry

fig

coffee

clove

toffee

pepper

jam

anise

smoke

chocolate

bell pepper

leather

cedar

black currant

sage

toast

plum

vanilla

pomegranate

tobacco

Isn't that a fun way to categorize the wines we drink?

Now it's time to crack open a bottle and give it a go. There are no wrong answers and the more you practice, the more you'll find the right language to describe your experience. It's a new language you're learning so be patient and have fun. Above all else, write everything down in the workbook pages following the structural elements breakdown. You can also sign up and join us for **High Five Wine Academy** for live wine scoring, wine education and community.

toniamcarthur.com

structural elements of wine

nose

Most of what we taste is influenced by our nose. That's why it is important to spend the time getting to know your glass first by identifying what you can smell. To do this, pour about an ounce or two of your wine. Holding it at a slight angle, pop your nose right into your glass, inhale deeply and really think about what your senses are telling you. Write it all down in your workbook and remember, there are no wrong answers here. Whatever you smell is whatever you smell.

acidity

Acidity is the ever-important quality that acts as a natural preservative. A wine is age worthy due to its acidity level, though, of course, it must be a very good quality wine to begin with. So what is acidity? What does it smell, taste and feel like on your nose or palate?

Detectable acidity on the nose can cause your mouth to water, especially for those of us with sensitive palates. Acidity will also make you pucker. Think of it as a sour taste. You can associate bright acidity with flavors like grapefruit, lemon or lime, for example.

There are words listed in your workbook portion to help you determine if each wine you try has acidity that your palate finds pleasing or not.

alcohol

You can have a little fun with this structural element. Once you've had some practice, try to guess the alcohol level of your wine. You really can't be off by any humongous margin since most wines range between 10% to 15%, and practice can help you become more familiar with how your palate identifies heat. With a well balanced wine it can be tricky to do - but not impossible. Remember to isolate each element as you go so you're only looking for alcohol, or only looking for acidity.

The sensations related to alcohol are heat and tingling. Only focus on these sensations for these next few sips of wine. Pay attention to the tip, sides and back of your tongue as well as the back of your throat. Allow a minute or two to pass as you sit and assess this element, especially if you're not sensitive to these sensations.

Where is your mouth tingling? Do you feel heat? Burning?

sweetness

This component of wine leaves a tingling on the very tip of your tongue. You might also detect an oily texture over the top of your tongue when a wine has some residual sugar, which is also referred to as viscosity.

tannin

You know that drying sensation you feel across your mouth after biting into a grape? That grippy, lip-stuck-to-your-teeth feeling is from the tannins in your wine. Tannins come from the skin, stems and pips or seeds of the grape. White wines don't typically give off that drying sensation since white wine grapes are pressed and the juice, or must, is separated from anything imparting those characteristics. Tannins can be bitter if done wrong, or pleasantly palatable when done right. Everything about wine has to do with balance! You want to be able to detect tannins, but not be smacked in the face with them. Much the same as any other single structural element.

Young wines tend to have bolder tannins while aged or mature wines can become soft and velvety.

body

Think of body like the difference between light and refreshing or heavy and rich. This is the weight of the wine. You might have a preference in general but there is always time to appreciate both depending on the season, the meal or even, your mood! A light-bodied wine will be refreshing and perfect for a pool party or a hammock in the shade on a hot day with a good book, examples which beg for something crisp like a Sauvignon Blanc or Pinot Grigio. On a cooler day or with a great big meal, you might opt for a full-bodied wine like an oaked Chardonnay or a Syrah.

layers or dimensions

A simple wine is one that only has a flavour or two. Something more complex will have many flavors that seem to follow one after another. A wine with many layers or dimensions is a complex wine.

Is this wine simple?
Is this wine complex?

length

Can you walk away from your glass of wine and still taste it a few minutes later? Two? Five?

Great length on your wine has you thinking about it long after you've had a sip. Great wine has great length, as it should! Anything worth another sip should always leave you wanting more.

finish

Describe your experience! What's left on your tastebuds? Are they dancing? Feeling stood up? What flavors are lingering? Sensations?

high five explanation

Here is where you **write** absolutely everything you think and feel about why you are scoring the wine as you are. Now that the technical stuff is out of the way taste your wine just for the fun of it. Did you taste the same things as you smelled? What was different? What is your overall view of this wine after breaking it down? Don't hold back — every thought you have, write it down.

And finally, give it your score out of **high five**.

Scored: ...-out-of-five

You did it!

You have become your own wine critic. Did you learn something new about your palate you didn't know before? Were you able to put words to a sensation you didn't have language for?

Keep practicing, you never know what you will find that will wow and dazzle your palate. Write down all of the good things and all of the bad because also knowing what you don't like will be especially helpful in the future when asking for wine recommendations or reading labels that offer insight to a wine's flavor profile.

The only thing left to do is flip to your table of contents at the beginning of this workbook and enter the wine you tasted on its corresponding page number and include the final score you gave it. This will help you easily find this wine down the road when it comes up in conversation or if you want to purchase it again.

See you for your next wine scoring!

Let's get social!

What was the first wine you scored with the **High Five Wine Scoring System**?

Follow me on Instagram and tag me in a post or in your stories with your first **High Five Wine Scoring System** score for **one free month** with the **High Five Wine Academy**!

@tonia.mcarthur
toniamcarthur.com

Name of Wine	Winey Wine	Region	Okanagan
Vintage of Wine	2021	Country	Canada
Grape Varietal	Wino Noir	Price	$26
Place of Purchase	Winey Wine Store	Date of Scoring	Jan 1, 2022

nose

- raspberry
- cherry
- tobacco
- vanilla
- spice
- mushroom
-
-
-
-

acidity

- bright
- sharp
- citrusy
- zesty
- mouth watering
- puckering
- sour
- tart
- crisp
- pungent

sweetness

dry		off dry		sweet	

tannins

- bitter
- astringent
- velvety
- silky
- smooth
- grippy
- N/A

alcohol

- heat sensation down my throat
- tingling on the tip of my tongue
-
-

13.5 %abv

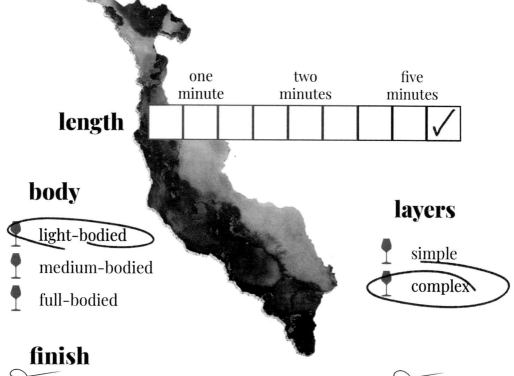

length

								✓

one minute   two minutes   five minutes

body

- (light-bodied)
- medium-bodied
- full-bodied

layers

- simple
- (complex)

finish

This wine seems to linger for quite a while. There's still a bit of fruit and earthiness on the palate, very nice.

explanation

It is a touch sweet for me but overall a nice wine. The nose was beautiful and those same notes were there to greet me on the palate as well. Overall I would enjoy this wine again but perhaps with some food. The sweetness wasn't off putting but I enjoy a little bit more of a dry Wino Noir for a sipping wine. I definitely wouldn't kick this wine out of bed!

score

three-out-of-five

Name of Wine		Region	
Vintage of Wine		Country	
Grape Varietal		Price	
Place of Purchase		Date of Scoring	

nose

acidity

bright

sharp

citrusy

zesty

mouth watering

puckering

sour

tart

crisp

pungent

sweetness

	dry			off dry			sweet		

tannins

bitter

astringent

velvety

silky

smooth

grippy

N/A

alcohol

...... %abv

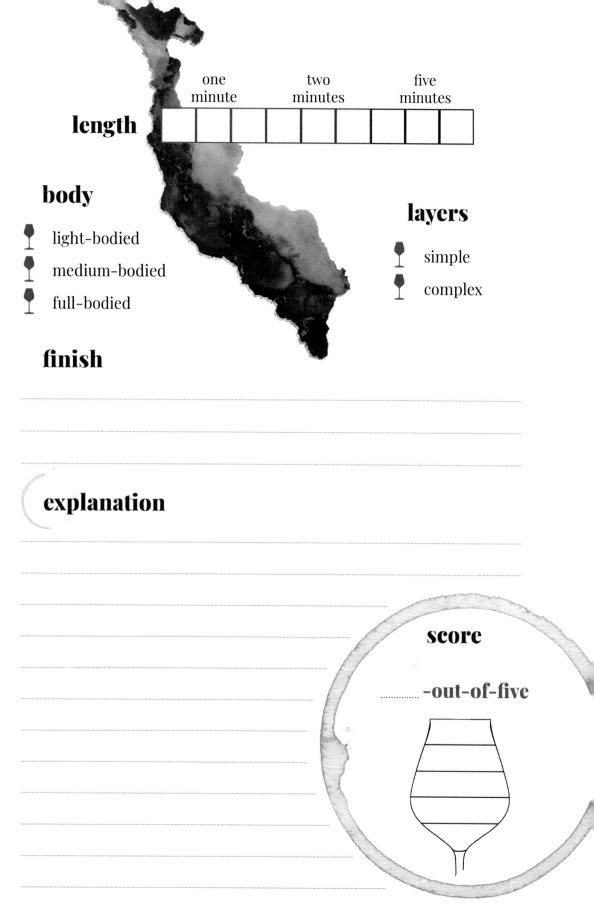

length

one minute		two minutes		five minutes		

body

🍷 light-bodied

🍷 medium-bodied

🍷 full-bodied

layers

🍷 simple

🍷 complex

finish

explanation

score

.... -out-of-five

Name of Wine		Region	
Vintage of Wine		Country	
Grape Varietal		Price	
Place of Purchase		Date of Scoring	

nose

acidity

bright

sharp

citrusy

zesty

mouth watering

puckering

sour

tart

crisp

pungent

sweetness

dry			off dry			sweet		

tannins

bitter

astringent

velvety

silky

smooth

grippy

N/A

alcohol

%abv

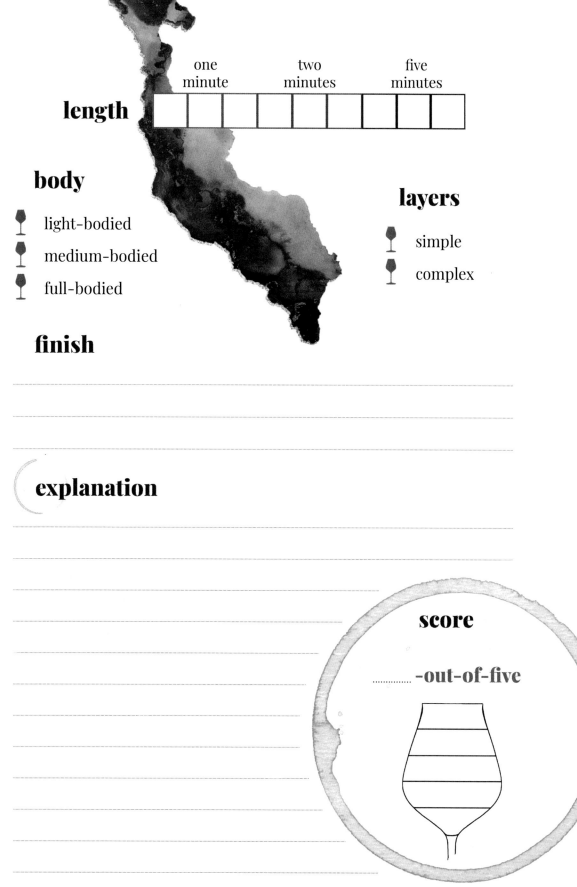

length

one minute			two minutes			five minutes		

body

🍷 light-bodied

🍷 medium-bodied

🍷 full-bodied

layers

🍷 simple

🍷 complex

finish

explanation

score

.............-out-of-five

Name of Wine		Region	
Vintage of Wine		Country	
Grape Varietal		Price	
Place of Purchase		Date of Scoring	

nose

acidity

- bright
- sharp
- citrusy
- zesty
- mouth watering
- puckering
- sour
- tart
- crisp
- pungent

sweetness

dry				off dry			sweet		

tannins

- bitter
- astringent
- velvety
- silky
- smooth
- grippy
- N/A

alcohol

_____ %abv

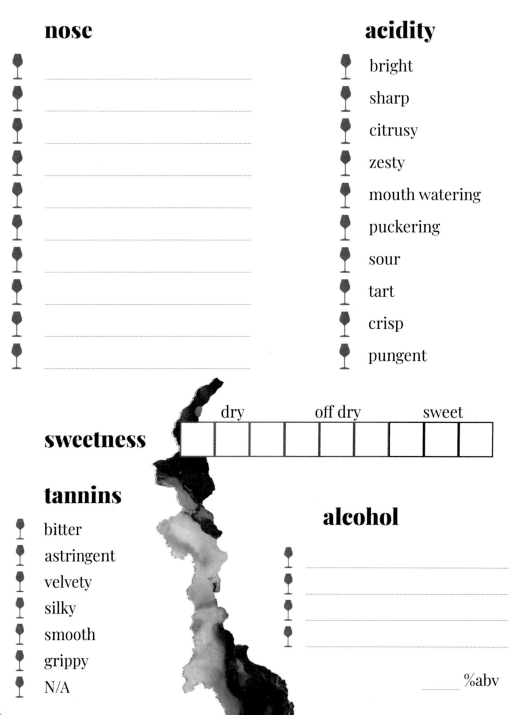

length

one minute		two minutes		five minutes				

body

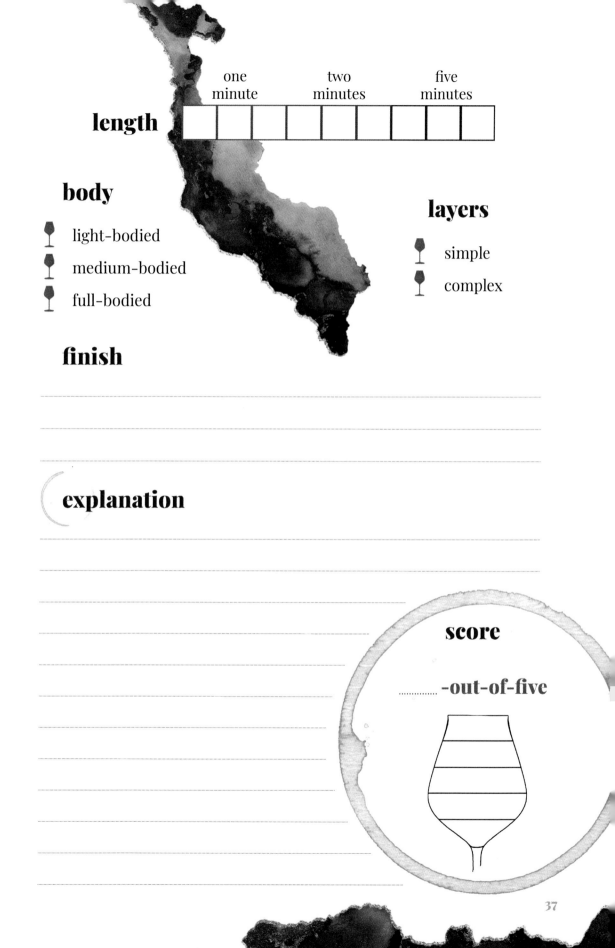 light-bodied

medium-bodied

full-bodied

layers

simple

complex

finish

explanation

score

.... -out-of-five

Name of Wine		Region	
Vintage of Wine		Country	
Grape Varietal		Price	
Place of Purchase		Date of Scoring	

nose

acidity

bright

sharp

citrusy

zesty

mouth watering

puckering

sour

tart

crisp

pungent

sweetness

	dry				off dry			sweet	

tannins

bitter

astringent

velvety

silky

smooth

grippy

N/A

alcohol

_____ %abv

length

	one minute			two minutes			five minutes	

body

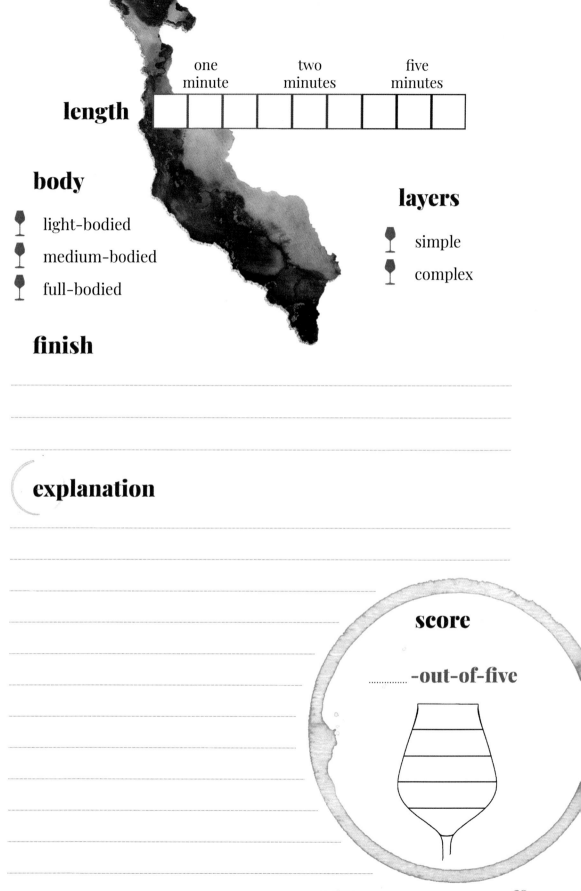

light-bodied

medium-bodied

full-bodied

layers

simple

complex

finish

....

....

explanation

....

....

....

....

....

....

....

....

....

score

.... -out-of-five

Name of Wine		Region	
Vintage of Wine		Country	
Grape Varietal		Price	
Place of Purchase		Date of Scoring	

nose

acidity

bright

sharp

citrusy

zesty

mouth watering

puckering

sour

tart

crisp

pungent

sweetness

dry   off dry   sweet

tannins

bitter

astringent

velvety

silky

smooth

grippy

N/A

alcohol

%abv

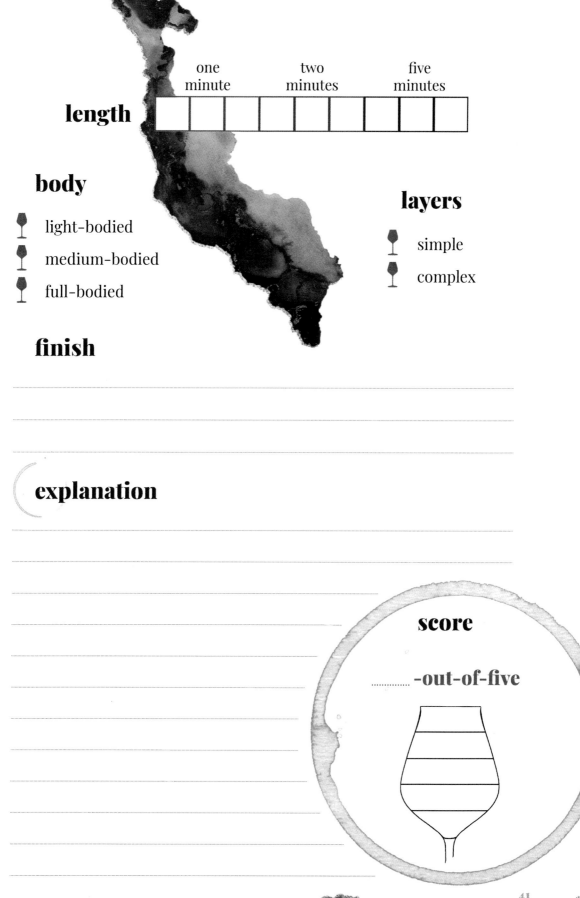

length

one minute			two minutes			five minutes		

body

🍷 light-bodied

🍷 medium-bodied

🍷 full-bodied

layers

🍷 simple

🍷 complex

finish

....

....

explanation

....

....

....

score

.... -out-of-five

Name of Wine		Region	
Vintage of Wine		Country	
Grape Varietal		Price	
Place of Purchase		Date of Scoring	

nose

acidity

bright

sharp

citrusy

zesty

mouth watering

puckering

sour

tart

crisp

pungent

sweetness

	dry			off dry			sweet	

tannins

bitter

astringent

velvety

silky

smooth

grippy

N/A

alcohol

%abv

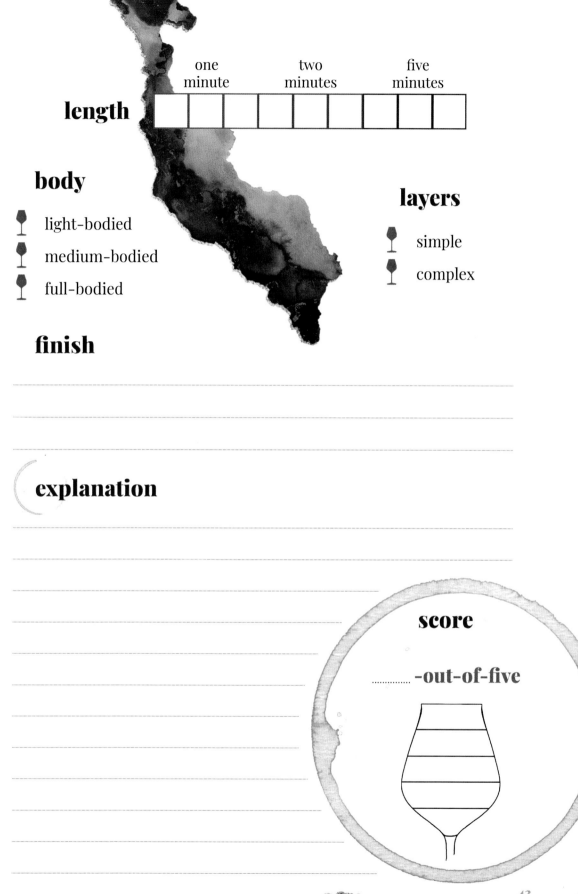

length

one minute			two minutes			five minutes		

body

- light-bodied
- medium-bodied
- full-bodied

layers

- simple
- complex

finish

explanation

score

.... -out-of-five

Name of Wine		Region	
Vintage of Wine		Country	
Grape Varietal		Price	
Place of Purchase		Date of Scoring	

nose

acidity

- bright
- sharp
- citrusy
- zesty
- mouth watering
- puckering
- sour
- tart
- crisp
- pungent

sweetness

dry   off dry   sweet

tannins

- bitter
- astringent
- velvety
- silky
- smooth
- grippy
- N/A

alcohol

_____ %abv

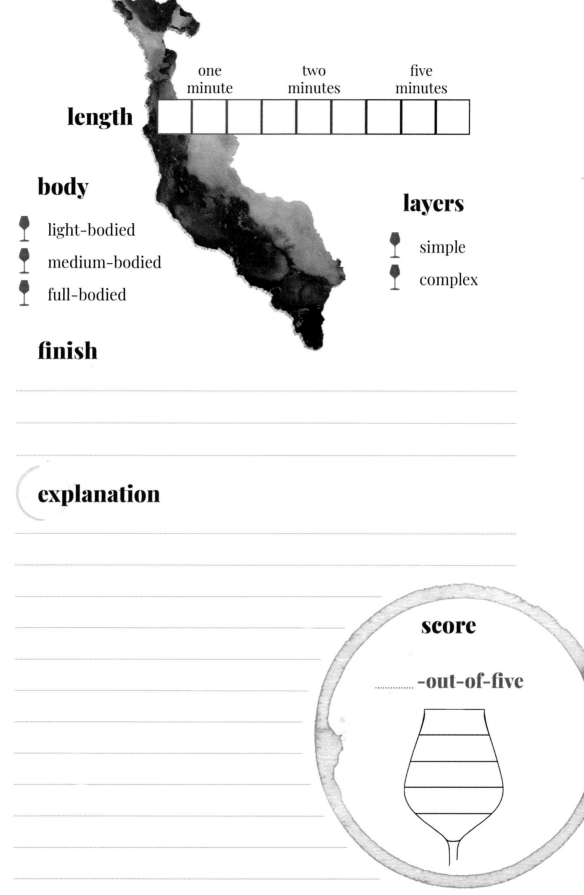

length

one minute			two minutes			five minutes		

body

light-bodied

medium-bodied

full-bodied

layers

simple

complex

finish

explanation

score

.... -out-of-five

Name of Wine		Region	
Vintage of Wine		Country	
Grape Varietal		Price	
Place of Purchase		Date of Scoring	

nose

acidity

🍷 bright

🍷 sharp

🍷 citrusy

🍷 zesty

🍷 mouth watering

🍷 puckering

🍷 sour

🍷 tart

🍷 crisp

🍷 pungent

sweetness

			dry			off dry			sweet	

tannins

🍷 bitter
🍷 astringent
🍷 velvety
🍷 silky
🍷 smooth
🍷 grippy
🍷 N/A

alcohol

_____ %abv

length

	one minute			two minutes			five minutes	

body

- light-bodied
- medium-bodied
- full-bodied

layers

- simple
- complex

finish

explanation

score

.... -out-of-five

47

Name of Wine		Region	
Vintage of Wine		Country	
Grape Varietal		Price	
Place of Purchase		Date of Scoring	

nose

acidity

- bright
- sharp
- citrusy
- zesty
- mouth watering
- puckering
- sour
- tart
- crisp
- pungent

sweetness

dry			off dry			sweet		

tannins

- bitter
- astringent
- velvety
- silky
- smooth
- grippy
- N/A

alcohol

%abv

48

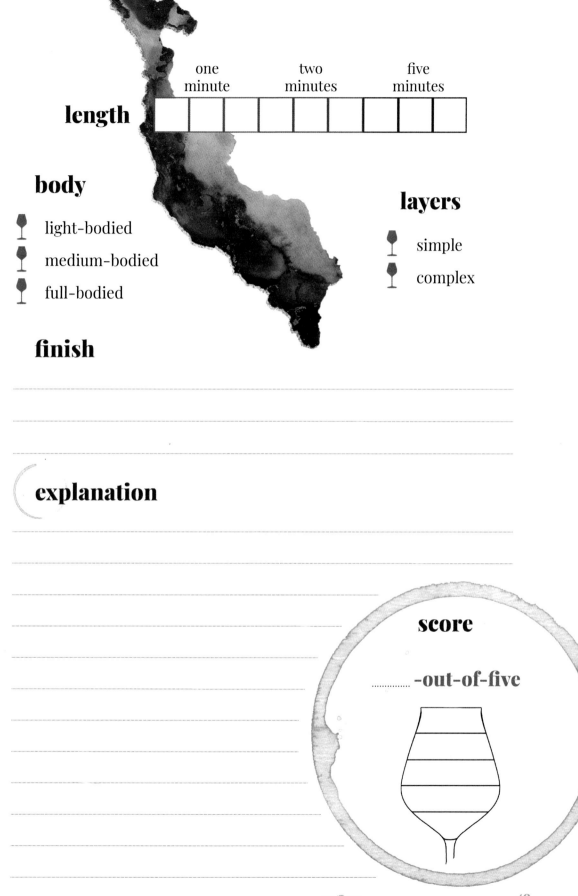

length

one minute		two minutes		five minutes

body

- light-bodied
- medium-bodied
- full-bodied

layers

- simple
- complex

finish

explanation

score

.... -out-of-five

Name of Wine		Region	
Vintage of Wine		Country	
Grape Varietal		Price	
Place of Purchase		Date of Scoring	

nose

acidity

bright

sharp

citrusy

zesty

mouth watering

puckering

sour

tart

crisp

pungent

sweetness

	dry			off dry			sweet		

tannins

bitter

astringent

velvety

silky

smooth

grippy

N/A

alcohol

_____ %abv

length

one minute		two minutes		five minutes			

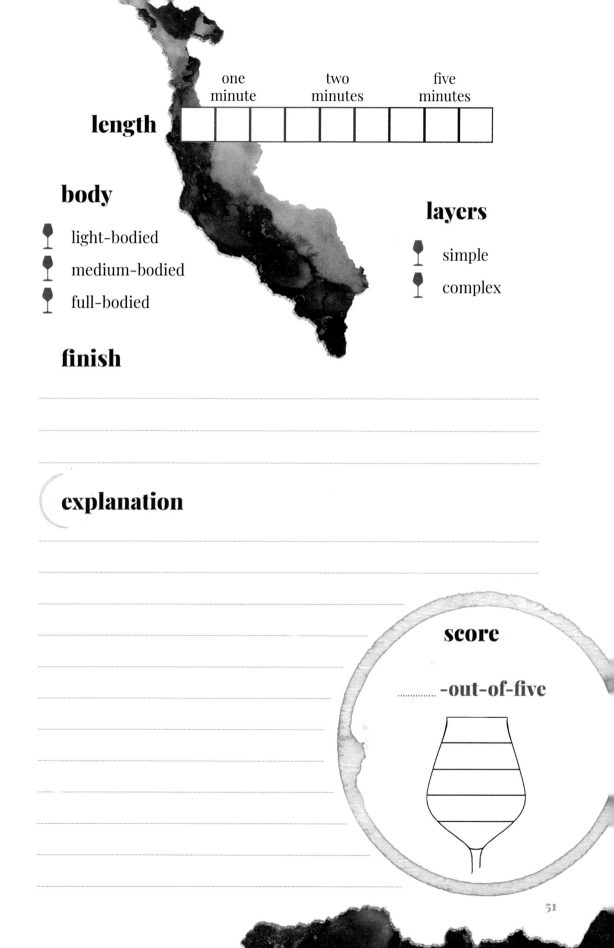

body

- light-bodied
- medium-bodied
- full-bodied

layers

- simple
- complex

finish

explanation

score

.... -out-of-five

Name of Wine		Region	
Vintage of Wine		Country	
Grape Varietal		Price	
Place of Purchase		Date of Scoring	

nose

acidity

bright

sharp

citrusy

zesty

mouth watering

puckering

sour

tart

crisp

pungent

sweetness

		dry			off dry			sweet	

tannins

bitter

astringent

velvety

silky

smooth

grippy

N/A

alcohol

%abv

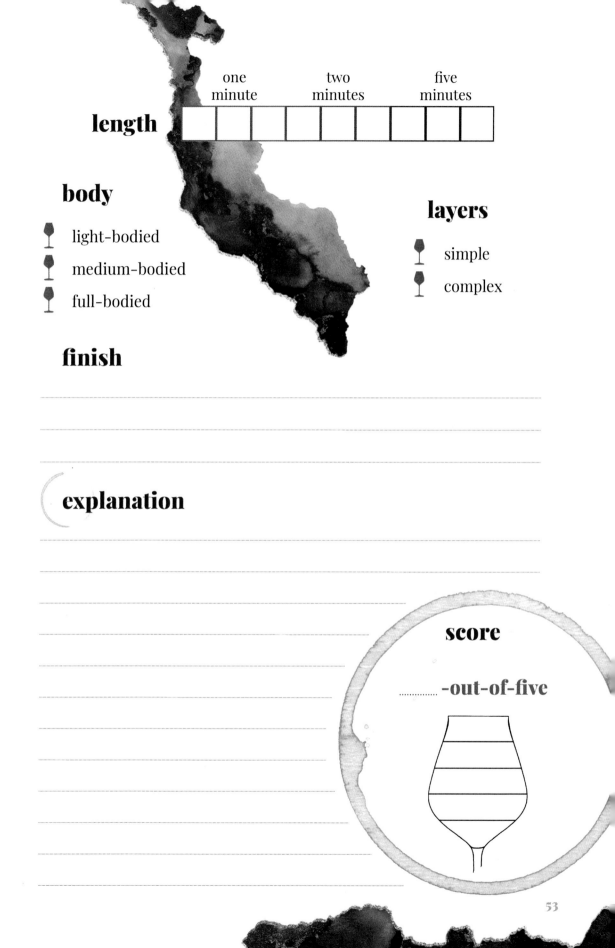

length

one minute			two minutes			five minutes		

body

- light-bodied
- medium-bodied
- full-bodied

layers

- simple
- complex

finish

explanation

score

.... -out-of-five

Name of Wine	....	Region	....
Vintage of Wine	....	Country	....
Grape Varietal	....	Price	....
Place of Purchase	....	Date of Scoring	....

nose

acidity

- bright
- sharp
- citrusy
- zesty
- mouth watering
- puckering
- sour
- tart
- crisp
- pungent

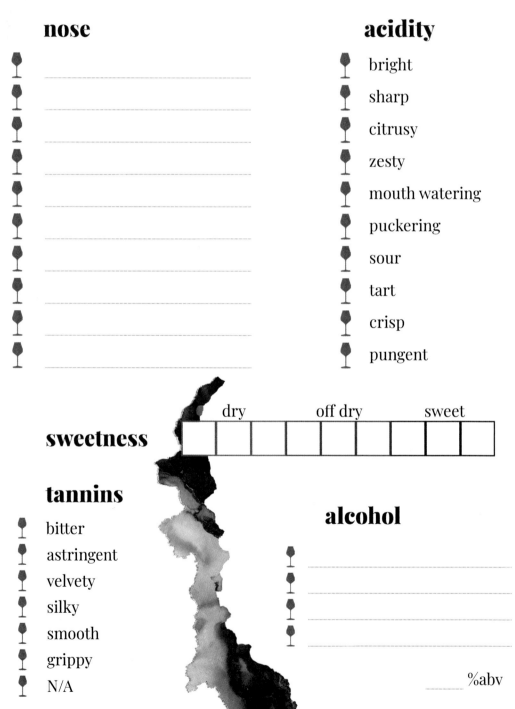

sweetness

dry   off dry   sweet

tannins

- bitter
- astringent
- velvety
- silky
- smooth
- grippy
- N/A

alcohol

.... %abv

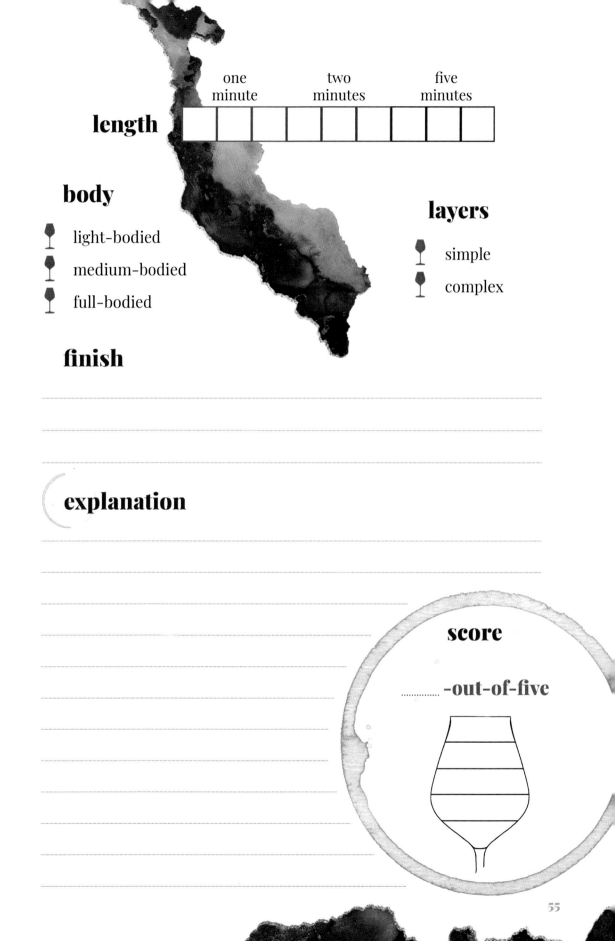

length

one minute   two minutes   five minutes

body

light-bodied

medium-bodied

full-bodied

layers

simple

complex

finish

explanation

score

.... -out-of-five

Name of Wine		Region	
Vintage of Wine		Country	
Grape Varietal		Price	
Place of Purchase		Date of Scoring	

nose

acidity

bright

sharp

citrusy

zesty

mouth watering

puckering

sour

tart

crisp

pungent

sweetness

	dry			off dry			sweet	

tannins

bitter
astringent
velvety
silky
smooth
grippy
N/A

alcohol

.... %abv

length

one minute			two minutes			five minutes		

body

🍷 light-bodied

🍷 medium-bodied

🍷 full-bodied

layers

🍷 simple

🍷 complex

finish

....

....

....

explanation

....

....

....

....

....

....

score

.... -out-of-five

....

....

Name of Wine		Region	
Vintage of Wine		Country	
Grape Varietal		Price	
Place of Purchase		Date of Scoring	

nose

acidity

- bright
- sharp
- citrusy
- zesty
- mouth watering
- puckering
- sour
- tart
- crisp
- pungent

sweetness

		dry			off dry			sweet	

tannins

- bitter
- astringent
- velvety
- silky
- smooth
- grippy
- N/A

alcohol

%abv

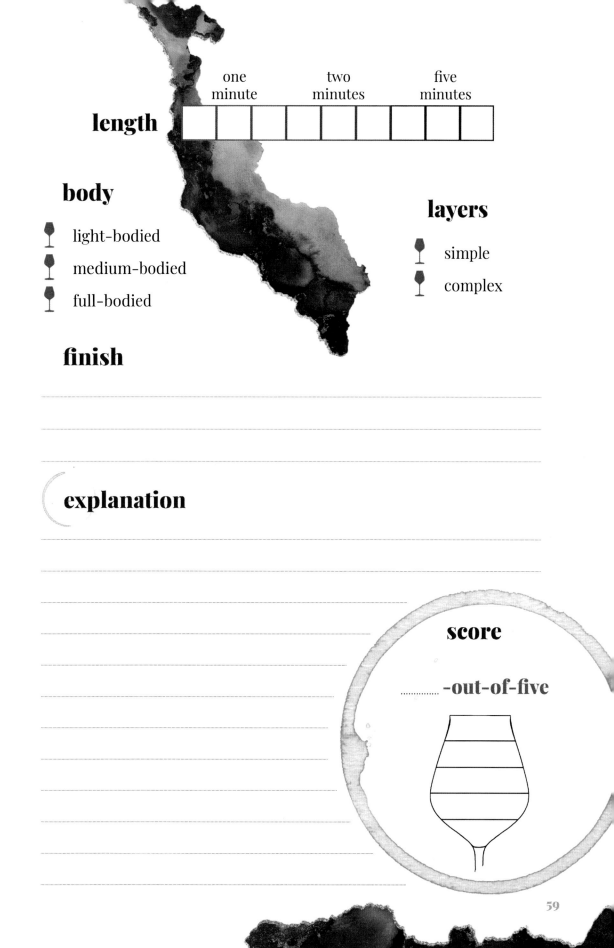

length

one minute   two minutes   five minutes

body

light-bodied

medium-bodied

full-bodied

layers

simple

complex

finish

explanation

score

.............-out-of-five

Name of Wine		Region	
Vintage of Wine		Country	
Grape Varietal		Price	
Place of Purchase		Date of Scoring	

nose

acidity

bright

sharp

citrusy

zesty

mouth watering

puckering

sour

tart

crisp

pungent

sweetness

dry | off dry | sweet

tannins

bitter

astringent

velvety

silky

smooth

grippy

N/A

alcohol

%abv

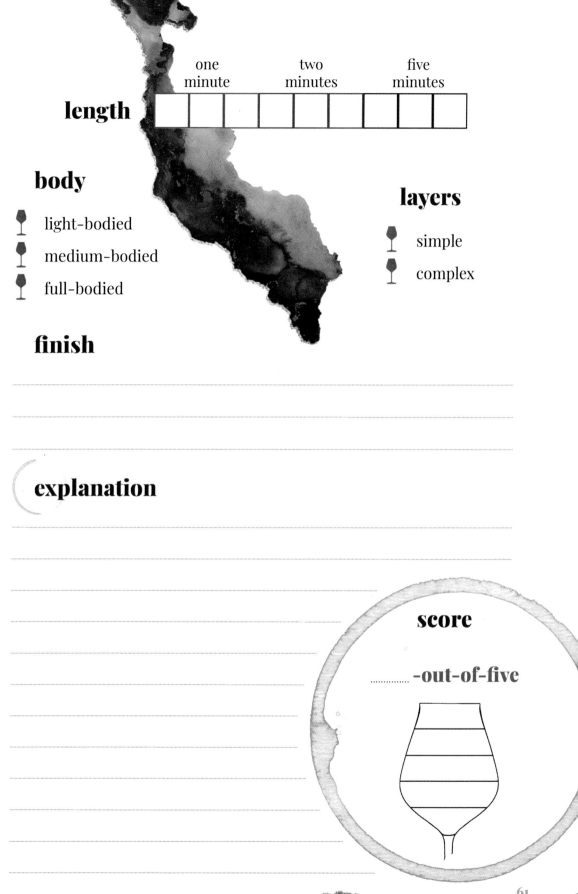

length

one minute			two minutes			five minutes		

body

🍷 light-bodied

🍷 medium-bodied

🍷 full-bodied

layers

🍷 simple

🍷 complex

finish

explanation

score

.............-out-of-five

61

Name of Wine		Region	
Vintage of Wine		Country	
Grape Varietal		Price	
Place of Purchase		Date of Scoring	

nose

acidity

bright

sharp

citrusy

zesty

mouth watering

puckering

sour

tart

crisp

pungent

sweetness

	dry			off dry			sweet		

tannins

bitter
astringent
velvety
silky
smooth
grippy
N/A

alcohol

_____ %abv

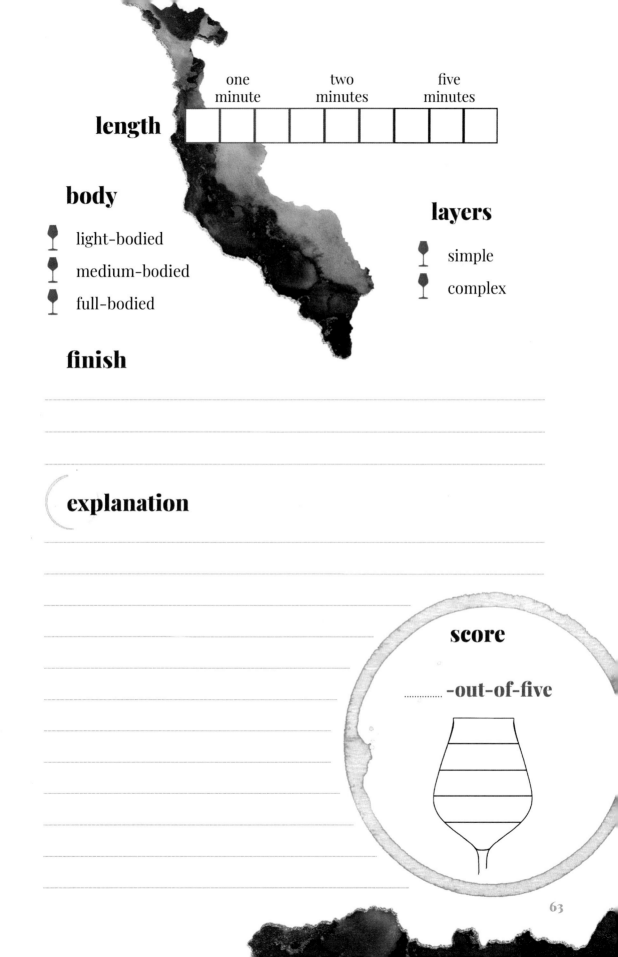

length

one minute			two minutes			five minutes		

body

light-bodied

medium-bodied

full-bodied

layers

simple

complex

finish

explanation

score

............-out-of-five

63

Name of Wine		Region	
Vintage of Wine		Country	
Grape Varietal		Price	
Place of Purchase		Date of Scoring	

nose

acidity

- bright
- sharp
- citrusy
- zesty
- mouth watering
- puckering
- sour
- tart
- crisp
- pungent

sweetness

dry				off dry			sweet	

tannins

- bitter
- astringent
- velvety
- silky
- smooth
- grippy
- N/A

alcohol

_____ %abv

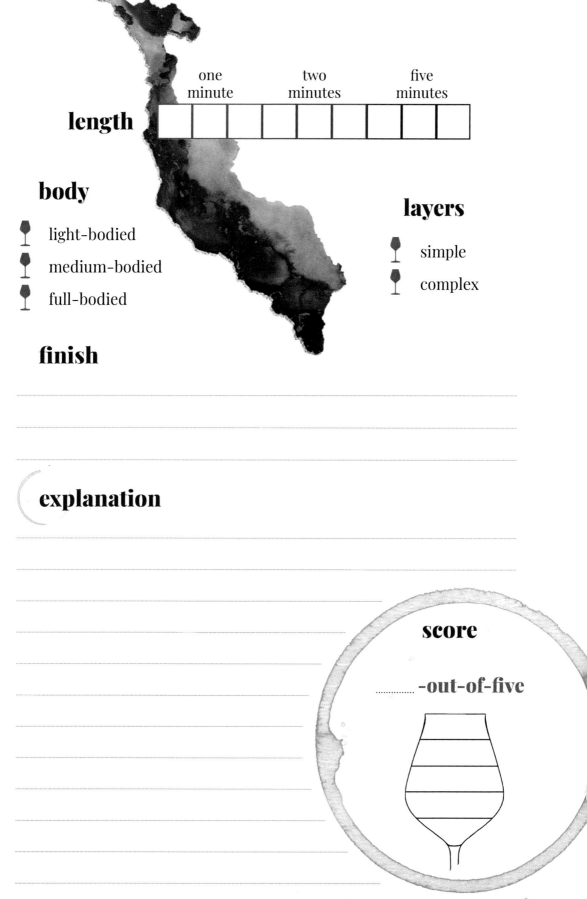

length

one minute   two minutes   five minutes

body

light-bodied

medium-bodied

full-bodied

layers

simple

complex

finish

explanation

score

............-out-of-five

65

Name of Wine		Region	
Vintage of Wine		Country	
Grape Varietal		Price	
Place of Purchase		Date of Scoring	

nose

acidity

bright

sharp

citrusy

zesty

mouth watering

puckering

sour

tart

crisp

pungent

sweetness

dry				off dry			sweet		

tannins

bitter

astringent

velvety

silky

smooth

grippy

N/A

alcohol

_____ %abv

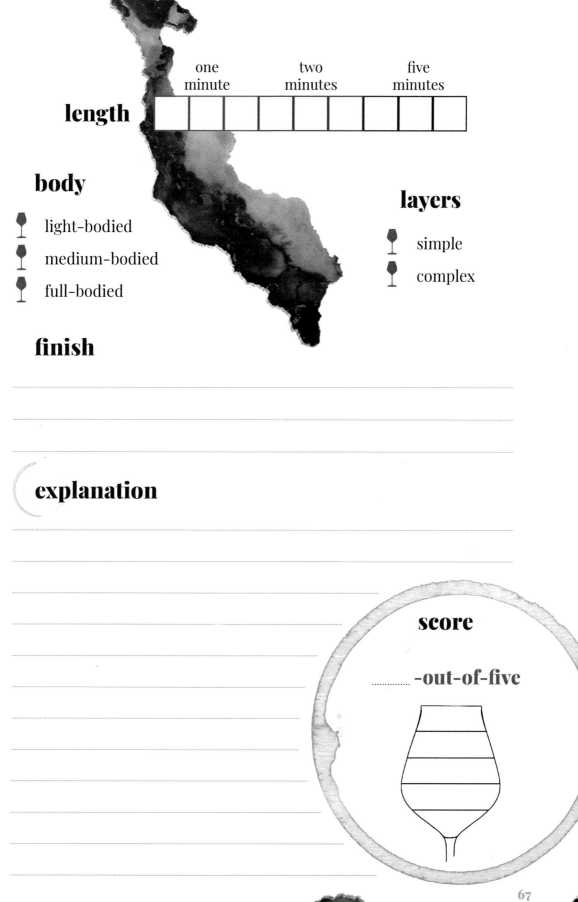

length

one minute			two minutes			five minutes		

body

light-bodied

medium-bodied

full-bodied

layers

simple

complex

finish

explanation

score

............-out-of-five

Name of Wine		Region	
Vintage of Wine		Country	
Grape Varietal		Price	
Place of Purchase		Date of Scoring	

nose

acidity

bright

sharp

citrusy

zesty

mouth watering

puckering

sour

tart

crisp

pungent

sweetness

	dry			off dry			sweet	

tannins

bitter

astringent

velvety

silky

smooth

grippy

N/A

alcohol

_____ %abv

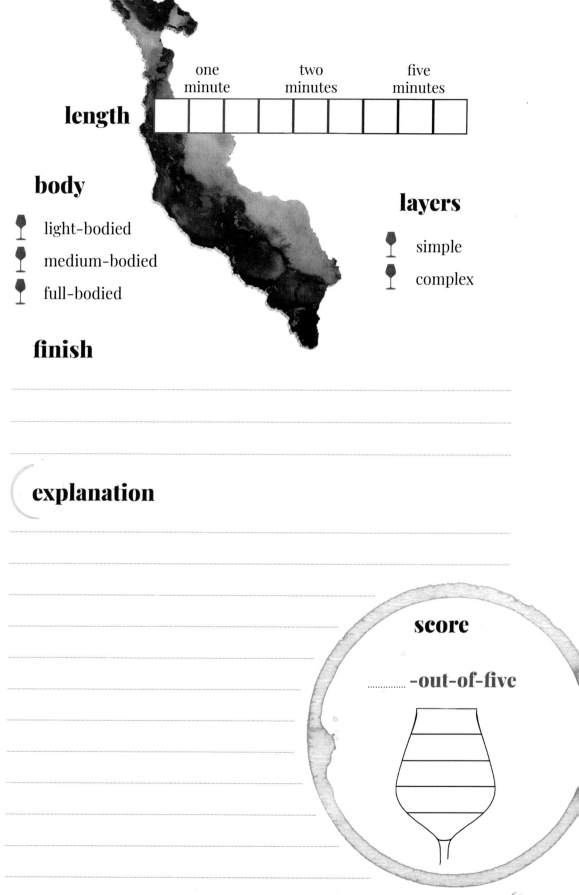

length

one minute   two minutes   five minutes

body

light-bodied

medium-bodied

full-bodied

layers

simple

complex

finish

explanation

score

.... -out-of-five

Name of Wine		Region	
Vintage of Wine		Country	
Grape Varietal		Price	
Place of Purchase		Date of Scoring	

nose

acidity

- bright
- sharp
- citrusy
- zesty
- mouth watering
- puckering
- sour
- tart
- crisp
- pungent

sweetness

dry			off dry			sweet		

tannins

- bitter
- astringent
- velvety
- silky
- smooth
- grippy
- N/A

alcohol

_____ %abv

70

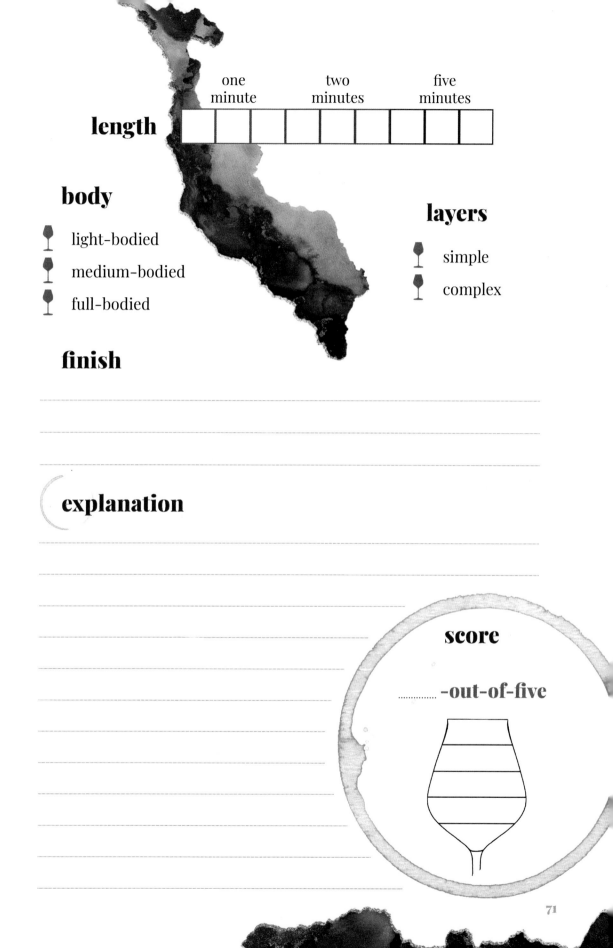

length

one minute   two minutes   five minutes

body

light-bodied

medium-bodied

full-bodied

layers

simple

complex

finish

explanation

score

............-out-of-five

Name of Wine		Region	
Vintage of Wine		Country	
Grape Varietal		Price	
Place of Purchase		Date of Scoring	

nose

acidity

- bright
- sharp
- citrusy
- zesty
- mouth watering
- puckering
- sour
- tart
- crisp
- pungent

sweetness

dry				off dry			sweet	

tannins

- bitter
- astringent
- velvety
- silky
- smooth
- grippy
- N/A

alcohol

_____ %abv

72

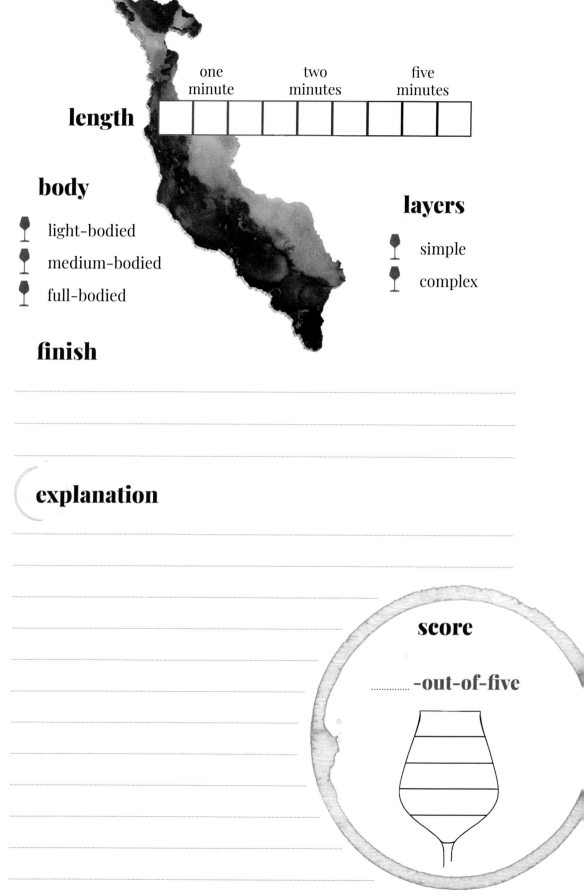

length

one
minute

two
minutes

five
minutes

body

light-bodied

medium-bodied

full-bodied

layers

simple

complex

finish

explanation

score

.... -out-of-five

Name of Wine		Region	
Vintage of Wine		Country	
Grape Varietal		Price	
Place of Purchase		Date of Scoring	

nose

acidity

- bright
- sharp
- citrusy
- zesty
- mouth watering
- puckering
- sour
- tart
- crisp
- pungent

sweetness

dry		off dry		sweet	

tannins

- bitter
- astringent
- velvety
- silky
- smooth
- grippy
- N/A

alcohol

_____ %abv

74

length

	one minute			two minutes			five minutes	

body

🍷 light-bodied

🍷 medium-bodied

🍷 full-bodied

layers

🍷 simple

🍷 complex

finish

....

....

explanation

....

....

....

....

....

score

.... -out-of-five

....

....

....

....

....

Name of Wine		Region	
Vintage of Wine		Country	
Grape Varietal		Price	
Place of Purchase		Date of Scoring	

nose

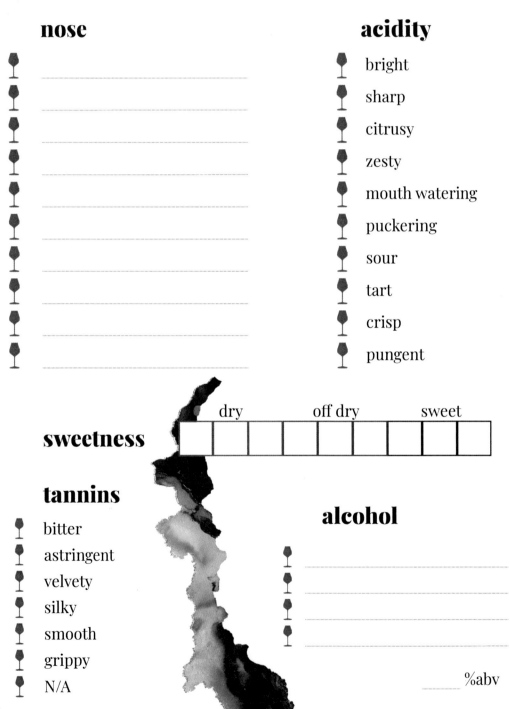

acidity

- bright
- sharp
- citrusy
- zesty
- mouth watering
- puckering
- sour
- tart
- crisp
- pungent

sweetness

dry			off dry			sweet		

tannins

- bitter
- astringent
- velvety
- silky
- smooth
- grippy
- N/A

alcohol

_____ %abv

length

one minute			two minutes			five minutes		

body

🍷 light-bodied

🍷 medium-bodied

🍷 full-bodied

layers

🍷 simple

🍷 complex

finish

explanation

score

.... -out-of-five

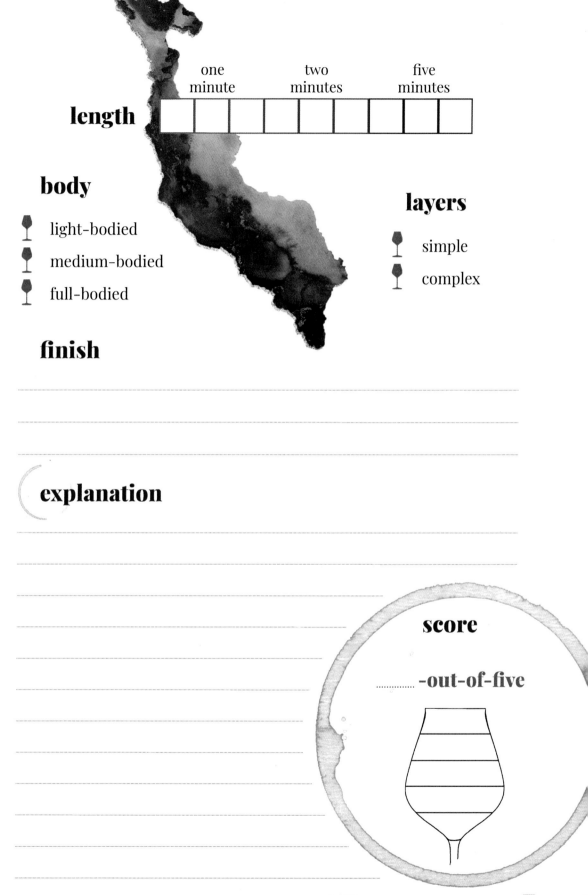

Name of Wine	**Region**	
Vintage of Wine	**Country**	
Grape Varietal	**Price**	
Place of Purchase	**Date of Scoring**	

nose

acidity

bright

sharp

citrusy

zesty

mouth watering

puckering

sour

tart

crisp

pungent

sweetness

dry   off dry   sweet

tannins

bitter

astringent

velvety

silky

smooth

grippy

N/A

alcohol

%abv

length

one minute   two minutes   five minutes

body

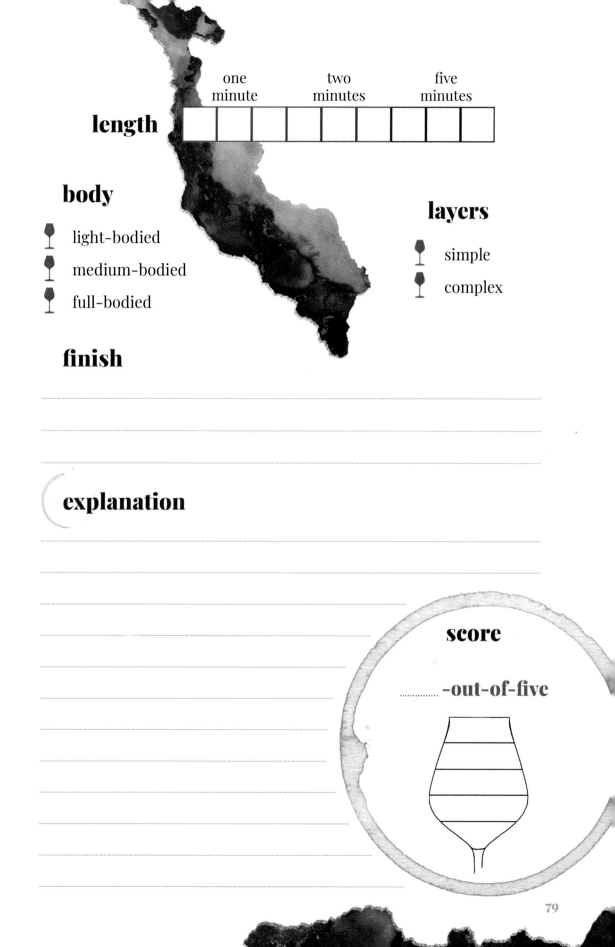 light-bodied

medium-bodied

full-bodied

layers

simple

complex

finish

....

....

....

explanation

....

....

....

....

....

....

....

score

.............-out-of-five

....

....

....

Name of Wine		Region	
Vintage of Wine		Country	
Grape Varietal		Price	
Place of Purchase		Date of Scoring	

nose

acidity

bright

sharp

citrusy

zesty

mouth watering

puckering

sour

tart

crisp

pungent

sweetness

	dry			off dry			sweet	

tannins

bitter

astringent

velvety

silky

smooth

grippy

N/A

alcohol

%abv

length

one minute			two minutes			five minutes		

body

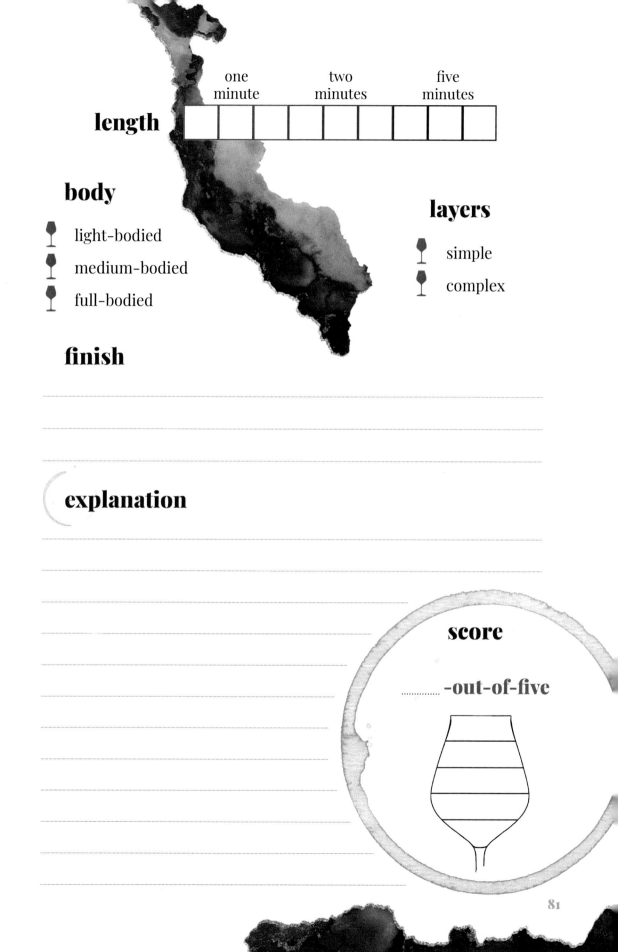

light-bodied

medium-bodied

full-bodied

layers

simple

complex

finish

explanation

score

.... -out-of-five

Name of Wine		Region	
Vintage of Wine		Country	
Grape Varietal		Price	
Place of Purchase		Date of Scoring	

nose

acidity

- bright
- sharp
- citrusy
- zesty
- mouth watering
- puckering
- sour
- tart
- crisp
- pungent

sweetness

	dry				off dry			sweet		

tannins

- bitter
- astringent
- velvety
- silky
- smooth
- grippy
- N/A

alcohol

%abv

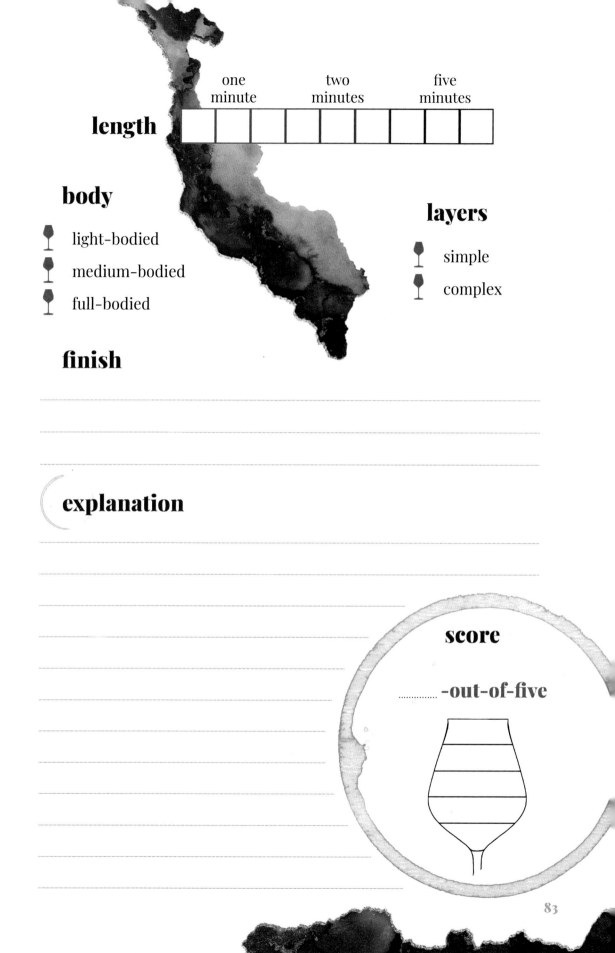

length

one minute   two minutes   five minutes

body

light-bodied

medium-bodied

full-bodied

layers

simple

complex

finish

explanation

score

............-out-of-five

Name of Wine		Region	
Vintage of Wine		Country	
Grape Varietal		Price	
Place of Purchase		Date of Scoring	

nose

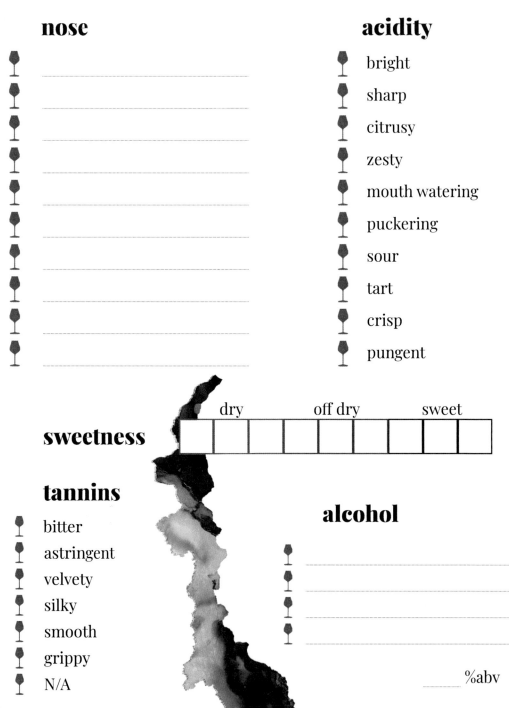

acidity

- bright
- sharp
- citrusy
- zesty
- mouth watering
- puckering
- sour
- tart
- crisp
- pungent

sweetness

	dry				off dry			sweet	

tannins

- bitter
- astringent
- velvety
- silky
- smooth
- grippy
- N/A

alcohol

%abv

length

one minute		two minutes			five minutes		

body

🍷 light-bodied

🍷 medium-bodied

🍷 full-bodied

layers

🍷 simple

🍷 complex

finish

....

....

explanation

....

....

....

....

....

....

....

....

score

.... -out-of-five

Name of Wine		Region	
Vintage of Wine		Country	
Grape Varietal		Price	
Place of Purchase		Date of Scoring	

nose

acidity

- bright
- sharp
- citrusy
- zesty
- mouth watering
- puckering
- sour
- tart
- crisp
- pungent

sweetness

dry				off dry			sweet	

tannins

- bitter
- astringent
- velvety
- silky
- smooth
- grippy
- N/A

alcohol

_____ %abv

length

one minute			two minutes			five minutes		

body

🍷 light-bodied

🍷 medium-bodied

🍷 full-bodied

layers

🍷 simple

🍷 complex

finish

....

....

explanation

....

....

....

....

....

score

.... -out-of-five

....

....

....

....

Name of Wine	....	Region	....
Vintage of Wine	....	Country	....
Grape Varietal	....	Price	....
Place of Purchase	....	Date of Scoring	....

nose

acidity

- bright
- sharp
- citrusy
- zesty
- mouth watering
- puckering
- sour
- tart
- crisp
- pungent

sweetness

dry				off dry			sweet	

tannins

- bitter
- astringent
- velvety
- silky
- smooth
- grippy
- N/A

alcohol

.... %abv

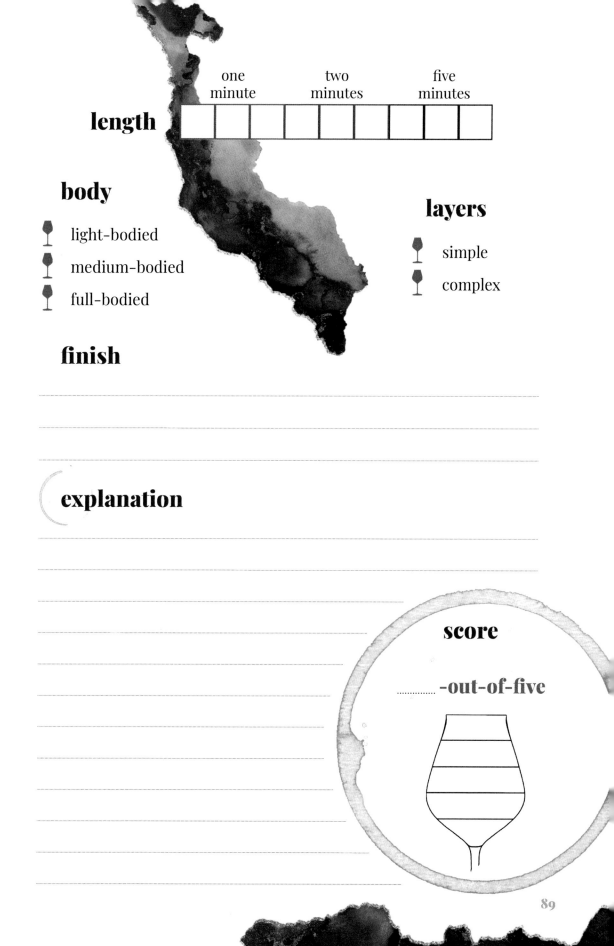

length

one minute   two minutes   five minutes

body

- light-bodied
- medium-bodied
- full-bodied

layers

- simple
- complex

finish

explanation

score

.... -out-of-five

Name of Wine		Region	
Vintage of Wine		Country	
Grape Varietal		Price	
Place of Purchase		Date of Scoring	

nose

acidity

- bright
- sharp
- citrusy
- zesty
- mouth watering
- puckering
- sour
- tart
- crisp
- pungent

sweetness

dry   off dry   sweet

tannins

- bitter
- astringent
- velvety
- silky
- smooth
- grippy
- N/A

alcohol

_____ %abv

length

one minute			two minutes			five minutes		

body

- 🍷 light-bodied
- 🍷 medium-bodied
- 🍷 full-bodied

layers

- 🍷 simple
- 🍷 complex

finish

....
....
....

explanation

....
....
....
....
....
....
....
....
....
....

score

.... -out-of-five

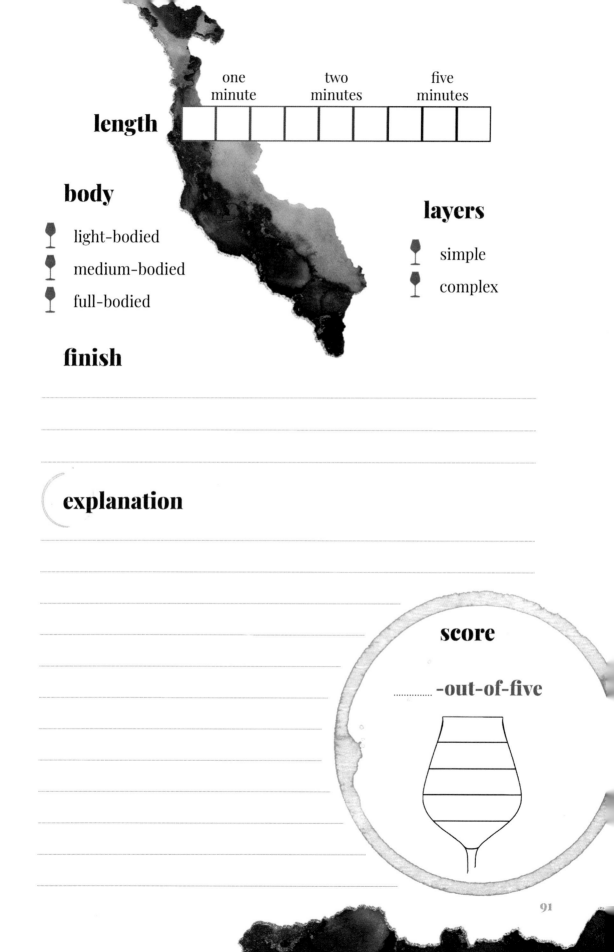

Name of Wine		Region	
Vintage of Wine		Country	
Grape Varietal		Price	
Place of Purchase		Date of Scoring	

nose

acidity

bright

sharp

citrusy

zesty

mouth watering

puckering

sour

tart

crisp

pungent

sweetness

	dry			off dry			sweet	

tannins

bitter
astringent
velvety
silky
smooth
grippy
N/A

alcohol

%abv

length

one minute · two minutes · five minutes

body

light-bodied

medium-bodied

full-bodied

layers

simple

complex

finish

explanation

score

.... -out-of-five

Name of Wine		Region	
Vintage of Wine		Country	
Grape Varietal		Price	
Place of Purchase		Date of Scoring	

nose

acidity

- bright
- sharp
- citrusy
- zesty
- mouth watering
- puckering
- sour
- tart
- crisp
- pungent

sweetness

dry   off dry   sweet

tannins

- bitter
- astringent
- velvety
- silky
- smooth
- grippy
- N/A

alcohol

_____ %abv

94

length

one
minute

two
minutes

five
minutes

body

light-bodied

medium-bodied

full-bodied

layers

simple

complex

finish

....

....

....

explanation

....

....

....

....

....

....

score

.... -out-of-five

....

....

....

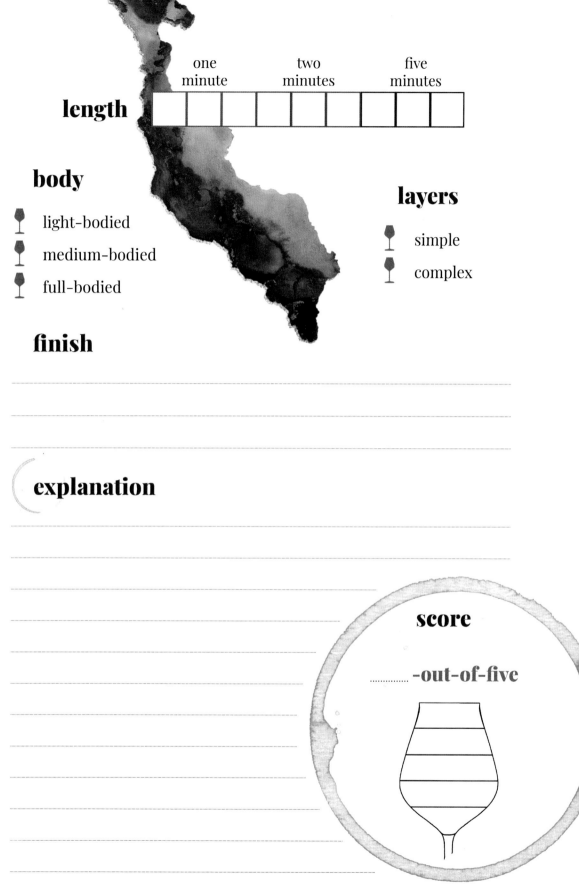

Name of Wine		Region	
Vintage of Wine		Country	
Grape Varietal		Price	
Place of Purchase		Date of Scoring	

nose

acidity

bright

sharp

citrusy

zesty

mouth watering

puckering

sour

tart

crisp

pungent

sweetness

dry				off dry			sweet	

tannins

bitter

astringent

velvety

silky

smooth

grippy

N/A

alcohol

%abv

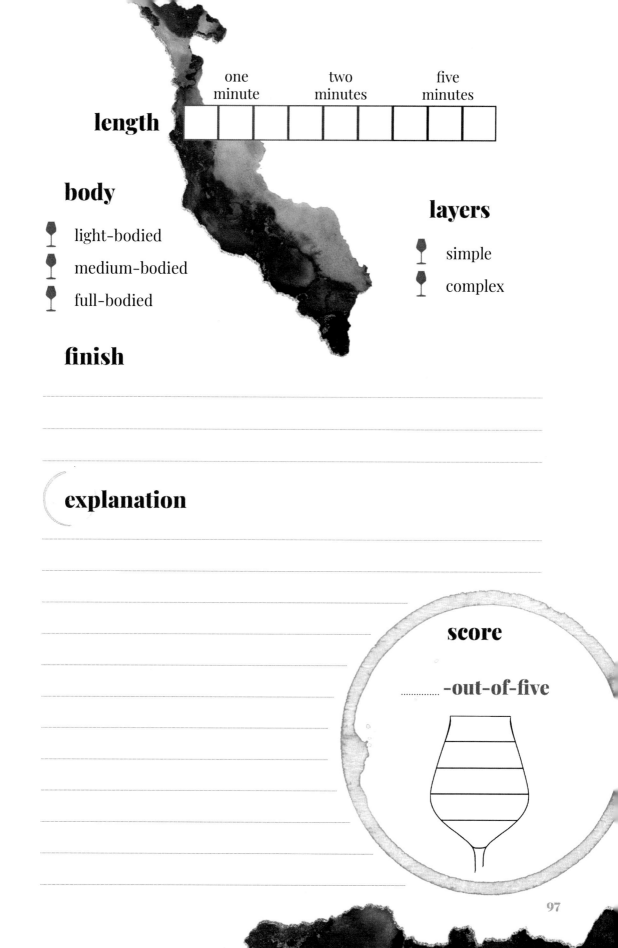

length

one minute			two minutes			five minutes		

body

- light-bodied
- medium-bodied
- full-bodied

layers

- simple
- complex

finish

explanation

score

.... -out-of-five

Name of Wine		Region	
Vintage of Wine		Country	
Grape Varietal		Price	
Place of Purchase		Date of Scoring	

nose

acidity

bright

sharp

citrusy

zesty

mouth watering

puckering

sour

tart

crisp

pungent

sweetness

dry			off dry			sweet		

tannins

bitter

astringent

velvety

silky

smooth

grippy

N/A

alcohol

_____ %abv

length

one minute   two minutes   five minutes

body

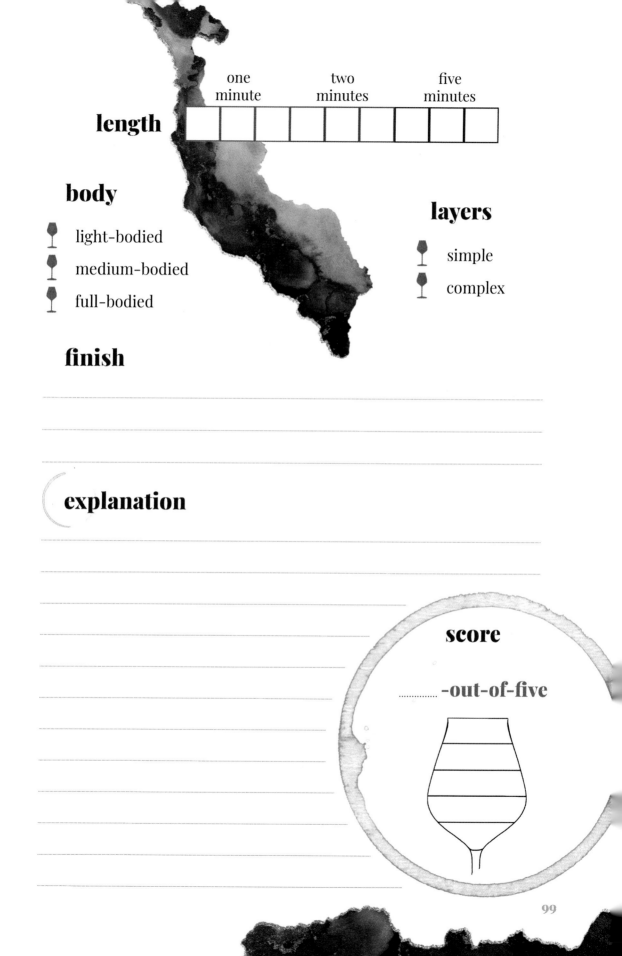

- light-bodied
- medium-bodied
- full-bodied

layers

- simple
- complex

finish

....

....

....

explanation

....

....

....

....

....

....

....

....

....

....

score

.... -out-of-five

Name of Wine		Region	
Vintage of Wine		Country	
Grape Varietal		Price	
Place of Purchase		Date of Scoring	

nose

acidity

- bright
- sharp
- citrusy
- zesty
- mouth watering
- puckering
- sour
- tart
- crisp
- pungent

sweetness

dry   off dry   sweet

tannins

- bitter
- astringent
- velvety
- silky
- smooth
- grippy
- N/A

alcohol

_____ %abv

length

one minute			two minutes			five minutes		

body

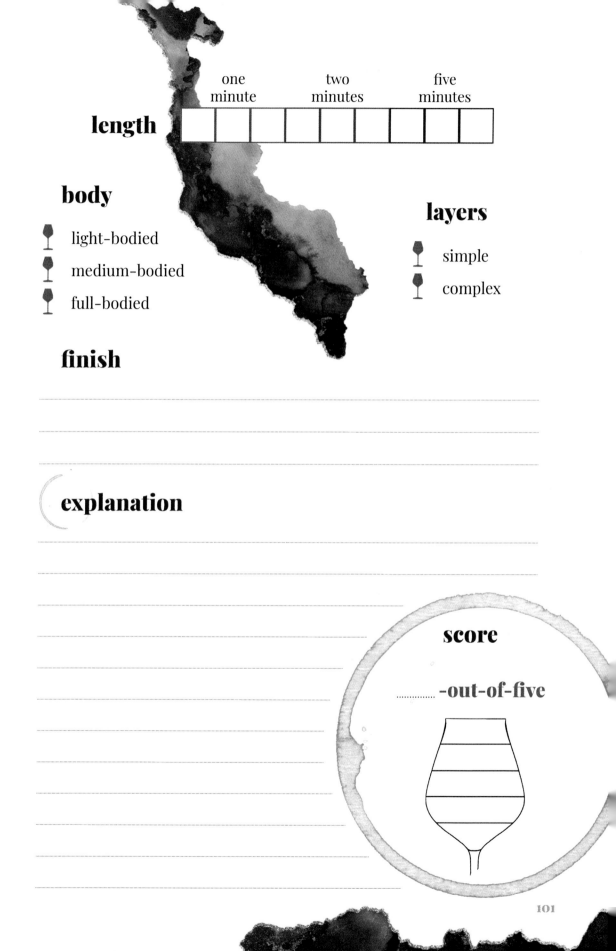

🍷 light-bodied

🍷 medium-bodied

🍷 full-bodied

layers

🍷 simple

🍷 complex

finish

explanation

score

.... -out-of-five

Name of Wine	....	Region	....
Vintage of Wine	....	Country	....
Grape Varietal	....	Price	....
Place of Purchase	....	Date of Scoring	....

nose

🍷 ....
🍷 ....
🍷 ....
🍷 ....
🍷 ....
🍷 ....
🍷 ....
🍷 ....
🍷 ....
🍷 ....

acidity

🍷 bright
🍷 sharp
🍷 citrusy
🍷 zesty
🍷 mouth watering
🍷 puckering
🍷 sour
🍷 tart
🍷 crisp
🍷 pungent

sweetness

dry				off dry			sweet		

tannins

🍷 bitter
🍷 astringent
🍷 velvety
🍷 silky
🍷 smooth
🍷 grippy
🍷 N/A

alcohol

🍷 ....
🍷 ....
🍷 ....
🍷 ....

.... %abv

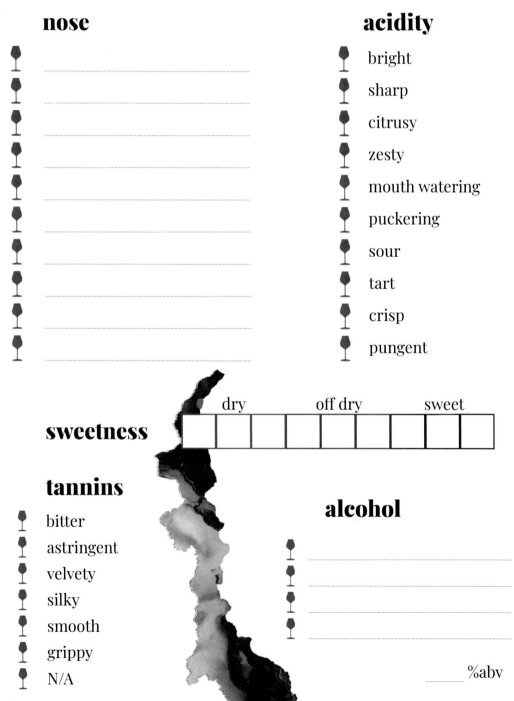

length

one minute   two minutes   five minutes

body

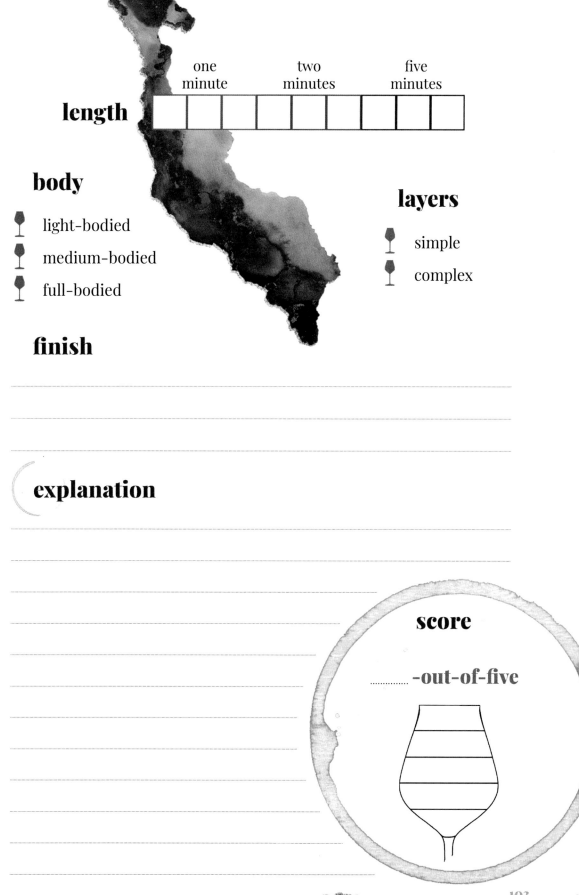

light-bodied

medium-bodied

full-bodied

layers

simple

complex

finish

explanation

score

............-out-of-five

Name of Wine		Region	
Vintage of Wine		Country	
Grape Varietal		Price	
Place of Purchase		Date of Scoring	

nose

acidity

bright

sharp

citrusy

zesty

mouth watering

puckering

sour

tart

crisp

pungent

sweetness

dry				off dry			sweet	

tannins

bitter
astringent
velvety
silky
smooth
grippy
N/A

alcohol

_____ %abv

length

one minute   two minutes   five minutes

body

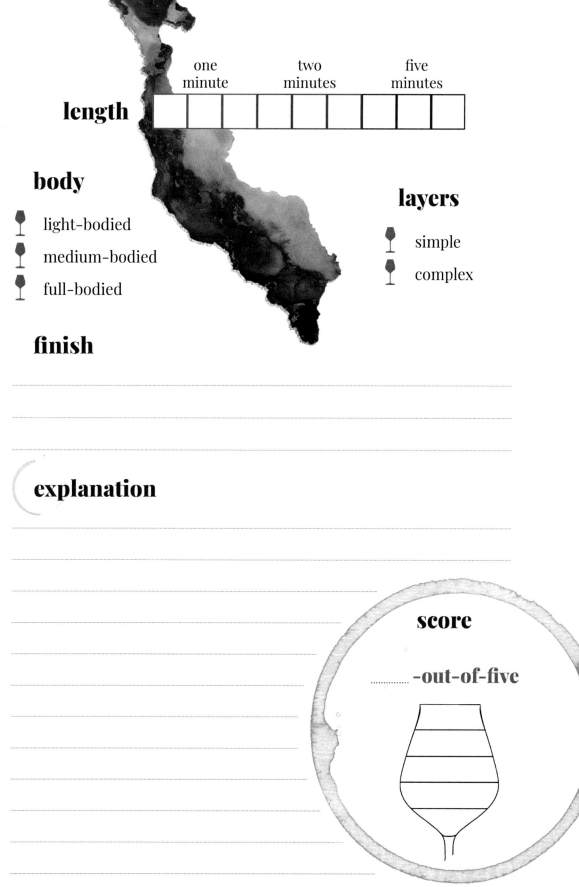

light-bodied

medium-bodied

full-bodied

layers

simple

complex

finish

explanation

score

.... -out-of-five

Name of Wine		Region	
Vintage of Wine		Country	
Grape Varietal		Price	
Place of Purchase		Date of Scoring	

nose

acidity

bright

sharp

citrusy

zesty

mouth watering

puckering

sour

tart

crisp

pungent

sweetness

	dry			off dry			sweet	

tannins

bitter
astringent
velvety
silky
smooth
grippy
N/A

alcohol

_____ %abv

106

length

one minute · two minutes · five minutes

body

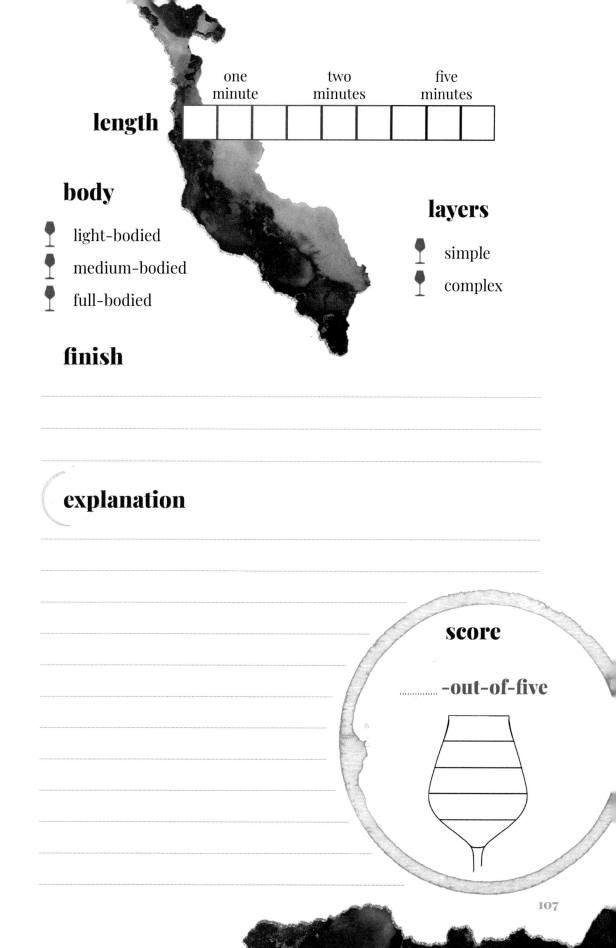

- light-bodied
- medium-bodied
- full-bodied

layers

- simple
- complex

finish

....

....

....

explanation

....

....

....

....

....

....

....

....

....

....

score

.... -out-of-five

Name of Wine	....	Region	....
Vintage of Wine	....	Country	....
Grape Varietal	....	Price	....
Place of Purchase	....	Date of Scoring	....

nose

acidity

🍷 bright

🍷 sharp

🍷 citrusy

🍷 zesty

🍷 mouth watering

🍷 puckering

🍷 sour

🍷 tart

🍷 crisp

🍷 pungent

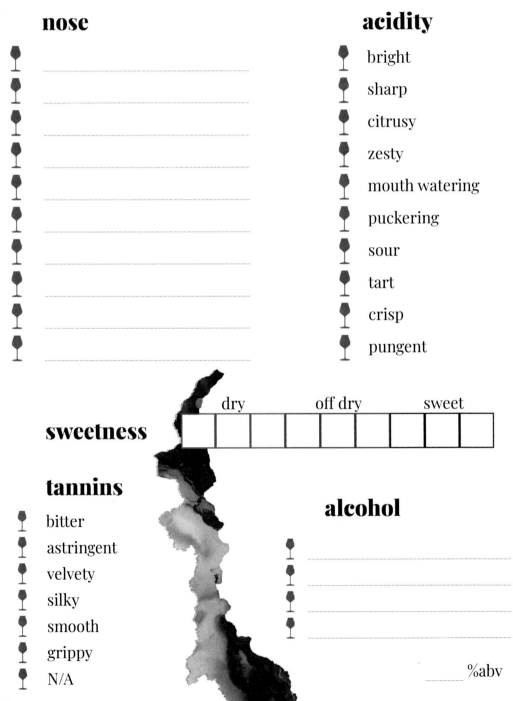

dry				off dry			sweet	

sweetness

tannins

🍷 bitter
🍷 astringent
🍷 velvety
🍷 silky
🍷 smooth
🍷 grippy
🍷 N/A

alcohol

🍷 ....
🍷 ....
🍷 ....
🍷 ....

.... %abv

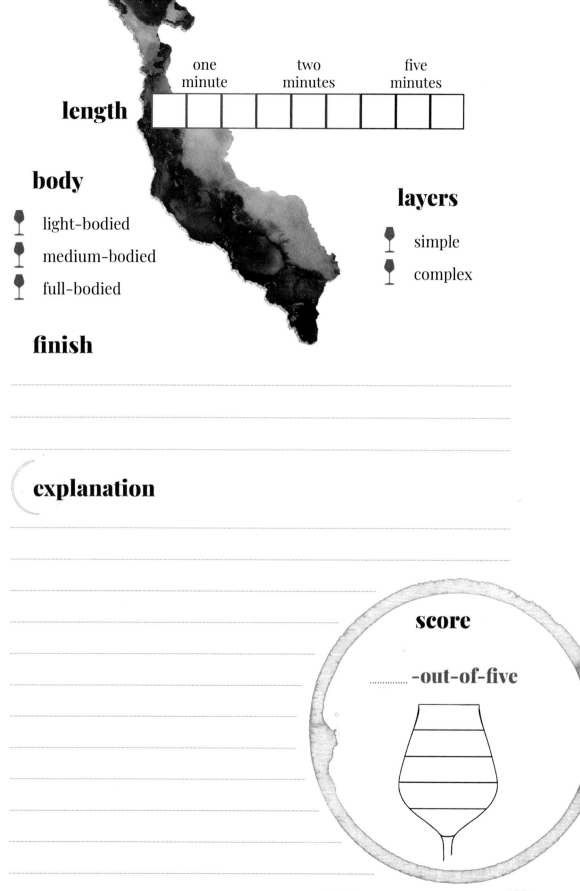

length

one minute   two minutes   five minutes

body

light-bodied

medium-bodied

full-bodied

layers

simple

complex

finish

explanation

score

.... -out-of-five

Name of Wine		Region	
Vintage of Wine		Country	
Grape Varietal		Price	
Place of Purchase		Date of Scoring	

nose

acidity

bright

sharp

citrusy

zesty

mouth watering

puckering

sour

tart

crisp

pungent

sweetness

	dry			off dry			sweet		

tannins

bitter
astringent
velvety
silky
smooth
grippy
N/A

alcohol

%abv

length

one minute | two minutes | five minutes

body

light-bodied
medium-bodied
full-bodied

layers

simple
complex

finish

....
....
....

explanation

....
....
....
....
....
....
....
....
....

score

.... -out-of-five

Name of Wine		Region	
Vintage of Wine		Country	
Grape Varietal		Price	
Place of Purchase		Date of Scoring	

nose

acidity

- bright
- sharp
- citrusy
- zesty
- mouth watering
- puckering
- sour
- tart
- crisp
- pungent

sweetness

	dry			off dry			sweet	

tannins

- bitter
- astringent
- velvety
- silky
- smooth
- grippy
- N/A

alcohol

_____ %abv

length

one minute   two minutes   five minutes

body

- light-bodied
- medium-bodied
- full-bodied

layers

- simple
- complex

finish

explanation

score

.... -out-of-five

Name of Wine		Region	
Vintage of Wine		Country	
Grape Varietal		Price	
Place of Purchase		Date of Scoring	

nose

acidity

- bright
- sharp
- citrusy
- zesty
- mouth watering
- puckering
- sour
- tart
- crisp
- pungent

sweetness

dry				off dry			sweet	

tannins

- bitter
- astringent
- velvety
- silky
- smooth
- grippy
- N/A

alcohol

_____ %abv

length

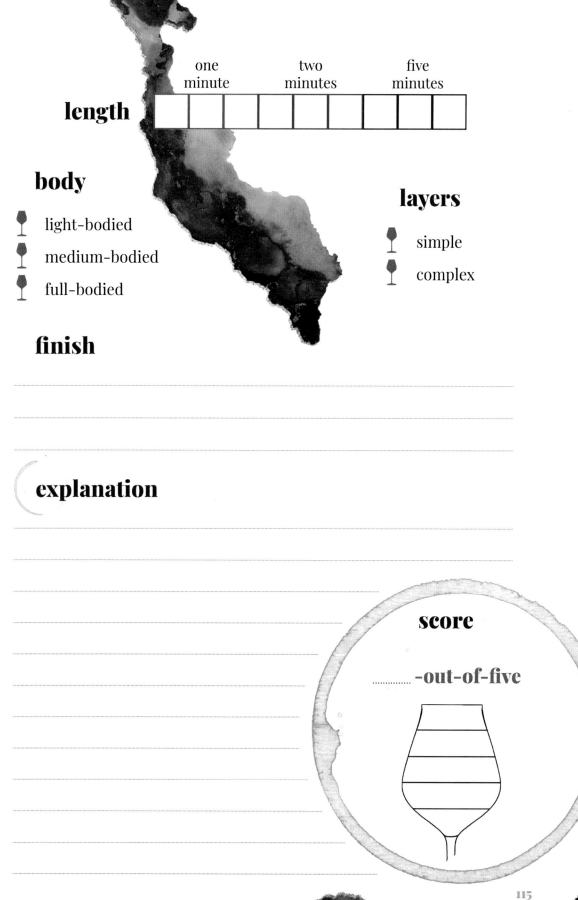

one minute   two minutes   five minutes

body

🍷 light-bodied

🍷 medium-bodied

🍷 full-bodied

layers

🍷 simple

🍷 complex

finish

explanation

score

.... -out-of-five

Name of Wine		Region	
Vintage of Wine		Country	
Grape Varietal		Price	
Place of Purchase		Date of Scoring	

nose

acidity

bright

sharp

citrusy

zesty

mouth watering

puckering

sour

tart

crisp

pungent

sweetness

dry				off dry			sweet	

tannins

bitter

astringent

velvety

silky

smooth

grippy

N/A

alcohol

%abv

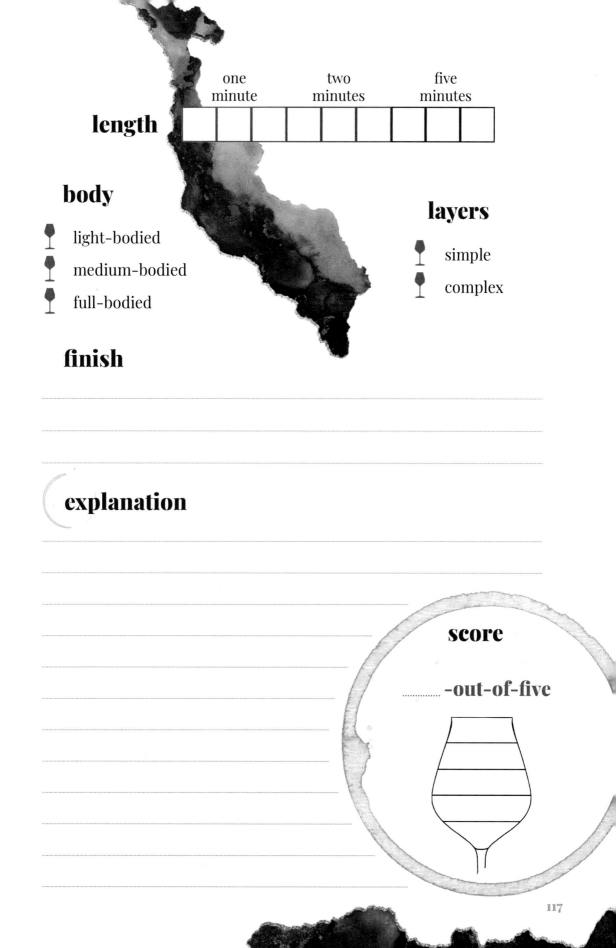

length

one minute   two minutes   five minutes

body

light-bodied

medium-bodied

full-bodied

layers

simple

complex

finish

explanation

score

.... -out-of-five

Name of Wine		Region	
Vintage of Wine		Country	
Grape Varietal		Price	
Place of Purchase		Date of Scoring	

nose

acidity

bright

sharp

citrusy

zesty

mouth watering

puckering

sour

tart

crisp

pungent

sweetness

dry				off dry			sweet	

tannins

bitter

astringent

velvety

silky

smooth

grippy

N/A

alcohol

%abv

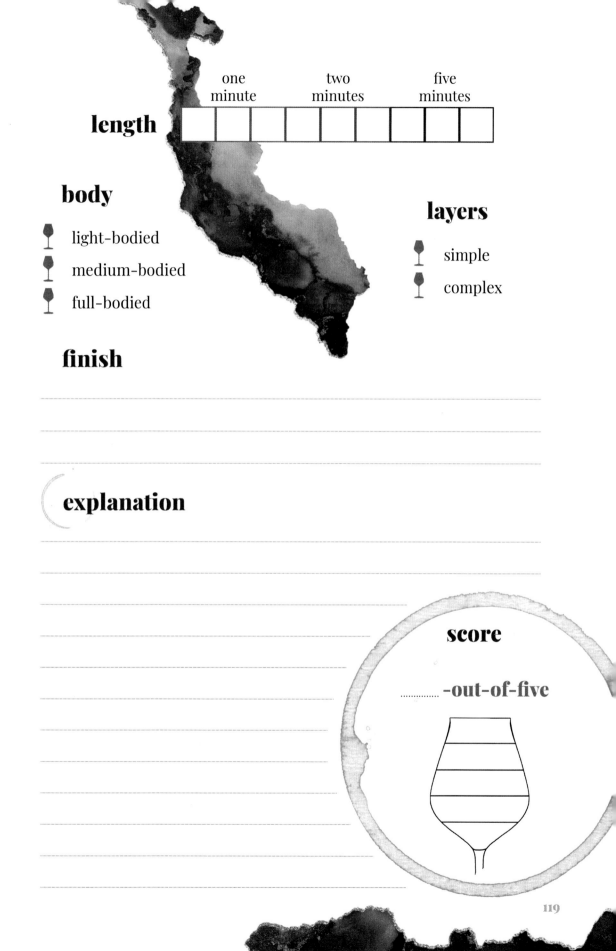

length

one minute   two minutes   five minutes

body

- light-bodied
- medium-bodied
- full-bodied

layers

- simple
- complex

finish

explanation

score

.... -out-of-five

Name of Wine		Region	
Vintage of Wine		Country	
Grape Varietal		Price	
Place of Purchase		Date of Scoring	

nose

acidity

bright

sharp

citrusy

zesty

mouth watering

puckering

sour

tart

crisp

pungent

sweetness

	dry			off dry			sweet	

tannins

bitter
astringent
velvety
silky
smooth
grippy
N/A

alcohol

_____ %abv

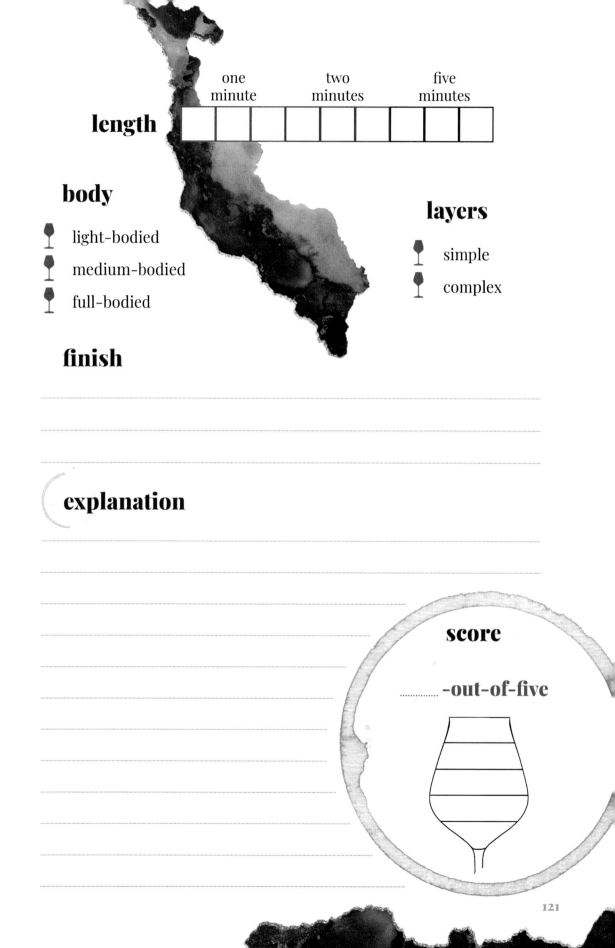

length

	one minute			two minutes			five minutes	

body

🍷 light-bodied

🍷 medium-bodied

🍷 full-bodied

layers

🍷 simple

🍷 complex

finish

explanation

score

.... -out-of-five

121

Name of Wine		Region	
Vintage of Wine		Country	
Grape Varietal		Price	
Place of Purchase		Date of Scoring	

nose

acidity

- bright
- sharp
- citrusy
- zesty
- mouth watering
- puckering
- sour
- tart
- crisp
- pungent

sweetness

dry			off dry			sweet		

tannins

- bitter
- astringent
- velvety
- silky
- smooth
- grippy
- N/A

alcohol

%abv

length

one minute			two minutes			five minutes		

body

light-bodied

medium-bodied

full-bodied

layers

simple

complex

finish

explanation

score

.... -out-of-five

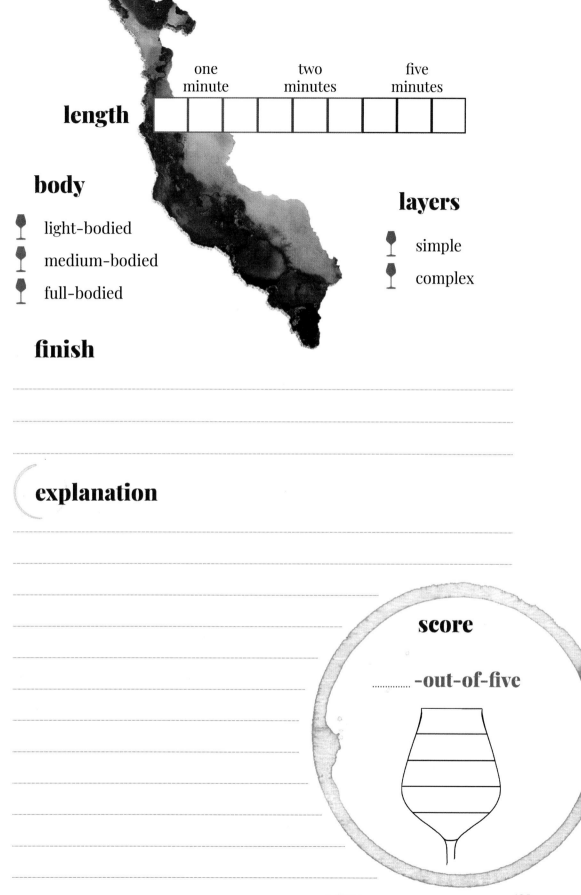

Name of Wine		Region	
Vintage of Wine		Country	
Grape Varietal		Price	
Place of Purchase		Date of Scoring	

nose

acidity

bright

sharp

citrusy

zesty

mouth watering

puckering

sour

tart

crisp

pungent

sweetness

dry   off dry   sweet

tannins

bitter

astringent

velvety

silky

smooth

grippy

N/A

alcohol

%abv

length

one minute			two minutes			five minutes		

body

🍷 light-bodied

🍷 medium-bodied

🍷 full-bodied

layers

🍷 simple

🍷 complex

finish

....

....

....

explanation

....

....

....

....

....

....

score

.... -out-of-five

....

....

....

Name of Wine		Region	
Vintage of Wine		Country	
Grape Varietal		Price	
Place of Purchase		Date of Scoring	

nose

acidity

- bright
- sharp
- citrusy
- zesty
- mouth watering
- puckering
- sour
- tart
- crisp
- pungent

sweetness

dry			off dry			sweet		

tannins

- bitter
- astringent
- velvety
- silky
- smooth
- grippy
- N/A

alcohol

%abv

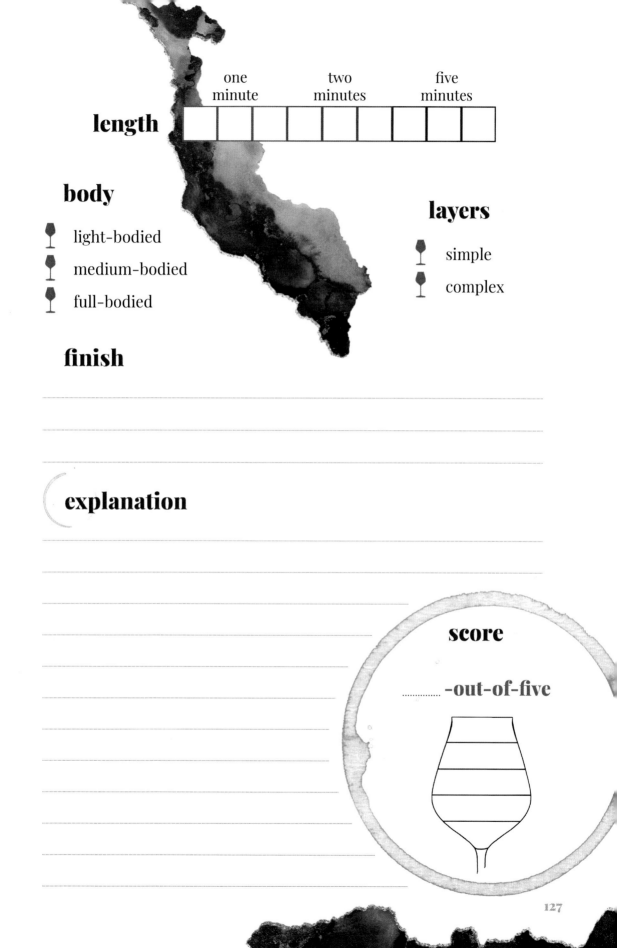

length

one minute			two minutes			five minutes		

body

- light-bodied
- medium-bodied
- full-bodied

layers

- simple
- complex

finish

explanation

score

.... -out-of-five

Name of Wine		Region	
Vintage of Wine		Country	
Grape Varietal		Price	
Place of Purchase		Date of Scoring	

nose

acidity

- bright
- sharp
- citrusy
- zesty
- mouth watering
- puckering
- sour
- tart
- crisp
- pungent

sweetness

	dry			off dry			sweet	

tannins

- bitter
- astringent
- velvety
- silky
- smooth
- grippy
- N/A

alcohol

_____ %abv

length

one minute			two minutes			five minutes		

body

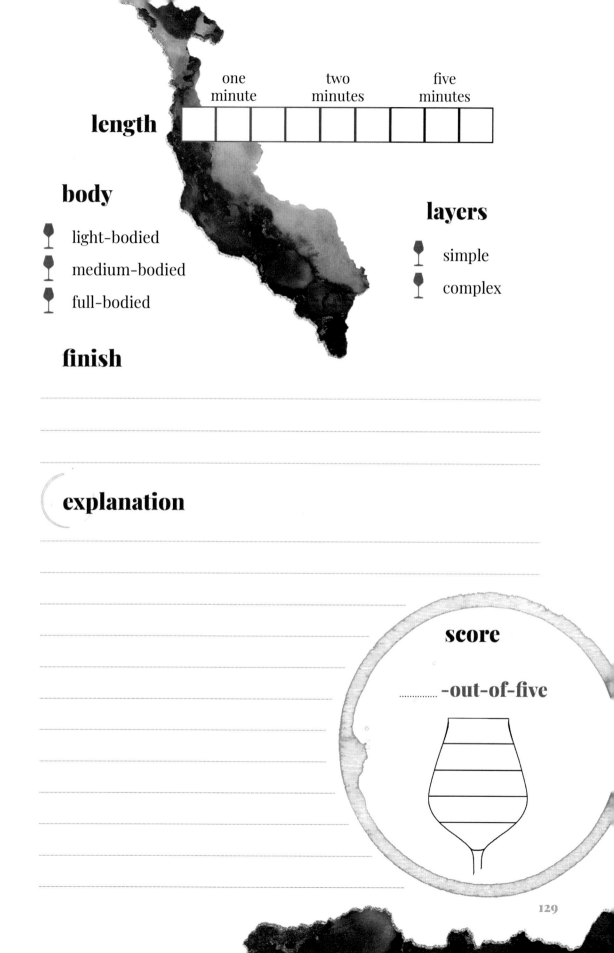

🍷 light-bodied

🍷 medium-bodied

🍷 full-bodied

layers

🍷 simple

🍷 complex

finish

explanation

score

.... -out-of-five

129

Name of Wine		Region	
Vintage of Wine		Country	
Grape Varietal		Price	
Place of Purchase		Date of Scoring	

nose

acidity

bright

sharp

citrusy

zesty

mouth watering

puckering

sour

tart

crisp

pungent

sweetness

	dry			off dry			sweet	

tannins

bitter

astringent

velvety

silky

smooth

grippy

N/A

alcohol

_____ %abv

length

one
minute two
minutes five
minutes

body

🍷 light-bodied

🍷 medium-bodied

🍷 full-bodied

layers

🍷 simple

🍷 complex

finish

explanation

score

............-out-of-five

Name of Wine		Region	
Vintage of Wine		Country	
Grape Varietal		Price	
Place of Purchase		Date of Scoring	

nose

acidity

- bright
- sharp
- citrusy
- zesty
- mouth watering
- puckering
- sour
- tart
- crisp
- pungent

sweetness

	dry			off dry			sweet		

tannins

- bitter
- astringent
- velvety
- silky
- smooth
- grippy
- N/A

alcohol

_____ %abv

length

one minute two minutes five minutes

body

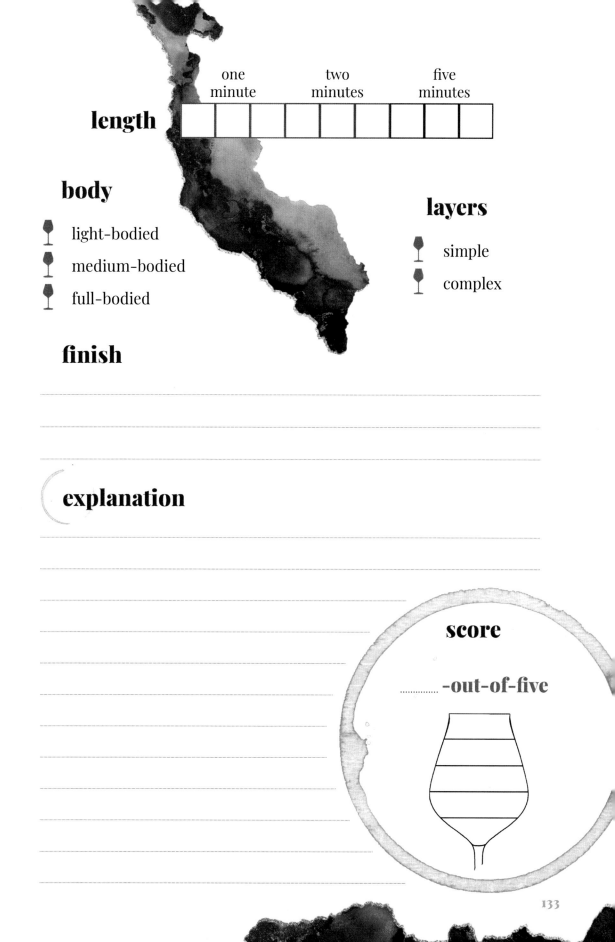 light-bodied

medium-bodied

full-bodied

layers

simple

complex

finish

explanation

score

.... -out-of-five

Name of Wine		Region	
Vintage of Wine		Country	
Grape Varietal		Price	
Place of Purchase		Date of Scoring	

nose

acidity

- bright
- sharp
- citrusy
- zesty
- mouth watering
- puckering
- sour
- tart
- crisp
- pungent

sweetness

dry				off dry			sweet	

tannins

- bitter
- astringent
- velvety
- silky
- smooth
- grippy
- N/A

alcohol

_____ %abv

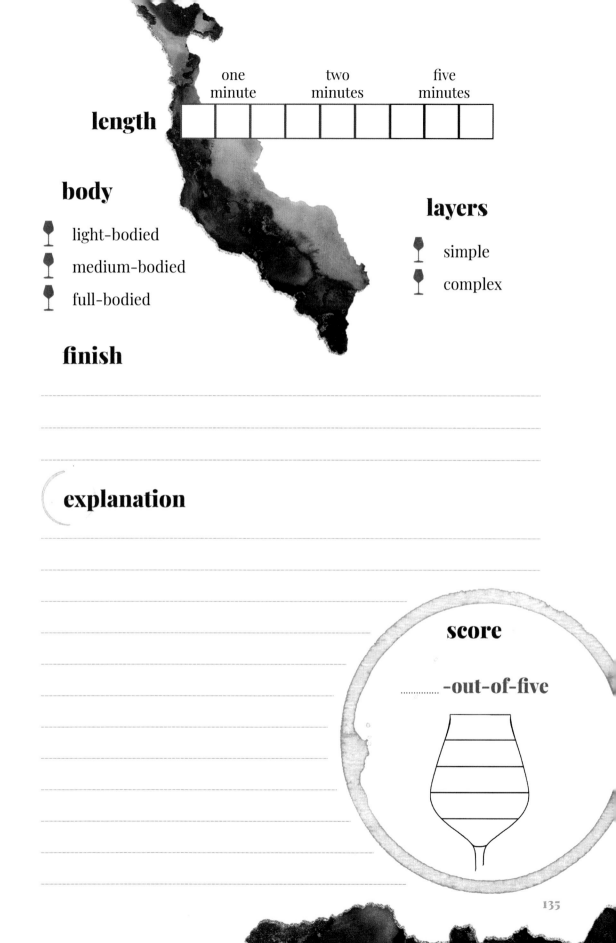

length

one minute | two minutes | five minutes

body

🍷 light-bodied
🍷 medium-bodied
🍷 full-bodied

layers

🍷 simple
🍷 complex

finish

explanation

score

............-out-of-five

Name of Wine		Region	
Vintage of Wine		Country	
Grape Varietal		Price	
Place of Purchase		Date of Scoring	

nose

acidity

bright

sharp

citrusy

zesty

mouth watering

puckering

sour

tart

crisp

pungent

dry   off dry   sweet

sweetness

tannins

bitter

astringent

velvety

silky

smooth

grippy

N/A

alcohol

%abv

length

one minute			two minutes			five minutes		

body

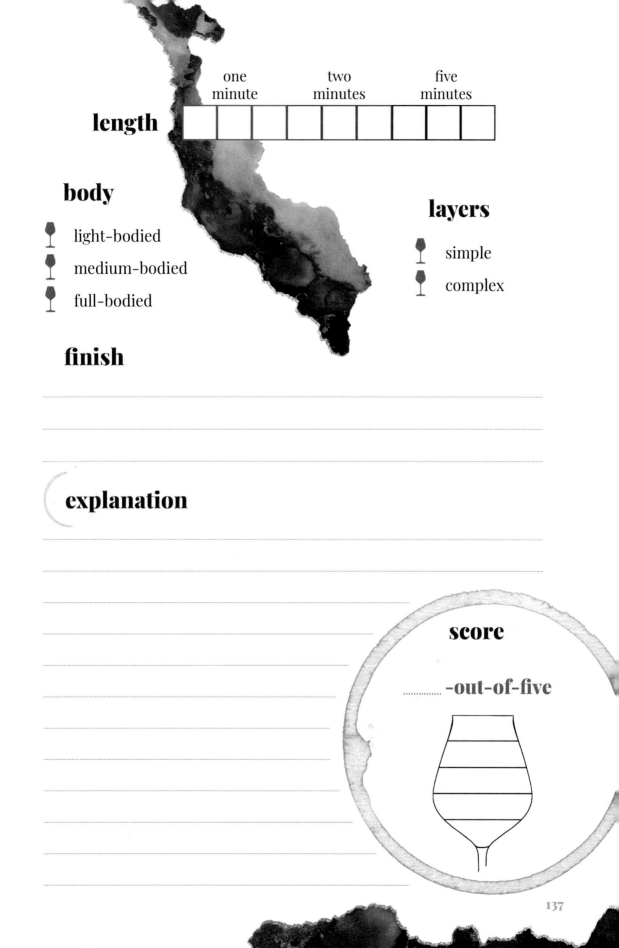

light-bodied

medium-bodied

full-bodied

layers

simple

complex

finish

explanation

score

.... -out-of-five

Name of Wine		Region	
Vintage of Wine		Country	
Grape Varietal		Price	
Place of Purchase		Date of Scoring	

nose

acidity

- bright
- sharp
- citrusy
- zesty
- mouth watering
- puckering
- sour
- tart
- crisp
- pungent

sweetness

	dry			off dry			sweet	

tannins

- bitter
- astringent
- velvety
- silky
- smooth
- grippy
- N/A

alcohol

_____ %abv

138

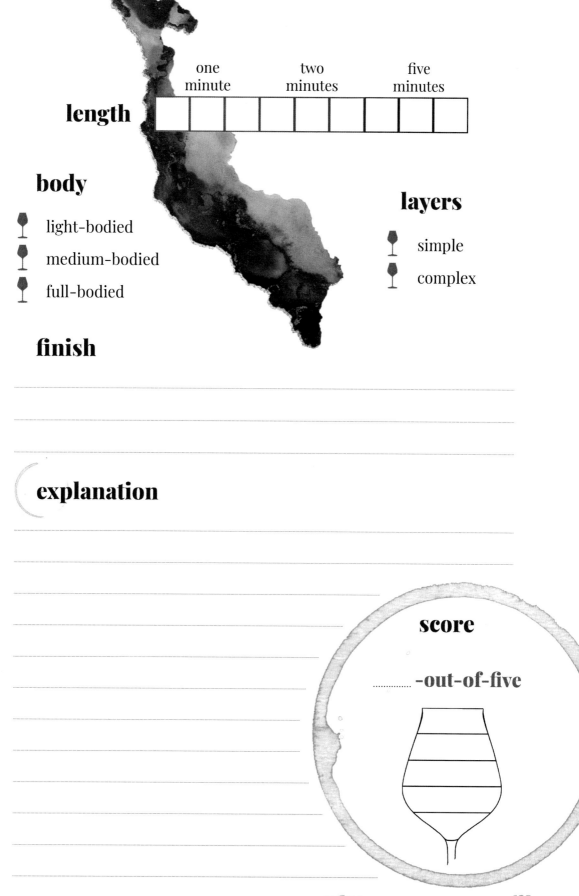

length

one minute			two minutes			five minutes		

body

🍷 light-bodied

🍷 medium-bodied

🍷 full-bodied

layers

🍷 simple

🍷 complex

finish

explanation

score

.... -out-of-five

Name of Wine		Region	
Vintage of Wine		Country	
Grape Varietal		Price	
Place of Purchase		Date of Scoring	

nose

acidity

bright

sharp

citrusy

zesty

mouth watering

puckering

sour

tart

crisp

pungent

sweetness

		dry			off dry			sweet	

tannins

bitter

astringent

velvety

silky

smooth

grippy

N/A

alcohol

.... %abv

length

one minute   two minutes   five minutes

body

🍷 light-bodied

🍷 medium-bodied

🍷 full-bodied

layers

🍷 simple

🍷 complex

finish

explanation

score

.... -out-of-five

Name of Wine		Region	
Vintage of Wine		Country	
Grape Varietal		Price	
Place of Purchase		Date of Scoring	

nose

acidity

- bright
- sharp
- citrusy
- zesty
- mouth watering
- puckering
- sour
- tart
- crisp
- pungent

sweetness

dry				off dry			sweet	

tannins

- bitter
- astringent
- velvety
- silky
- smooth
- grippy
- N/A

alcohol

_____ %abv

length

	one minute			two minutes			five minutes		

body

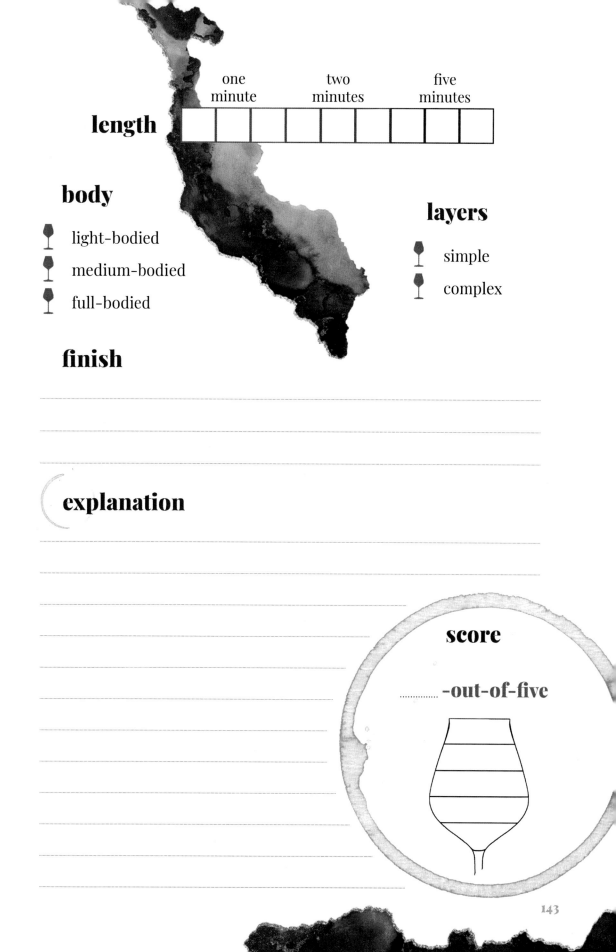

- light-bodied
- medium-bodied
- full-bodied

layers

- simple
- complex

finish

explanation

score

............-out-of-five

Name of Wine	....	Region	....
Vintage of Wine	....	Country	....
Grape Varietal	....	Price	....
Place of Purchase	....	Date of Scoring	....

nose

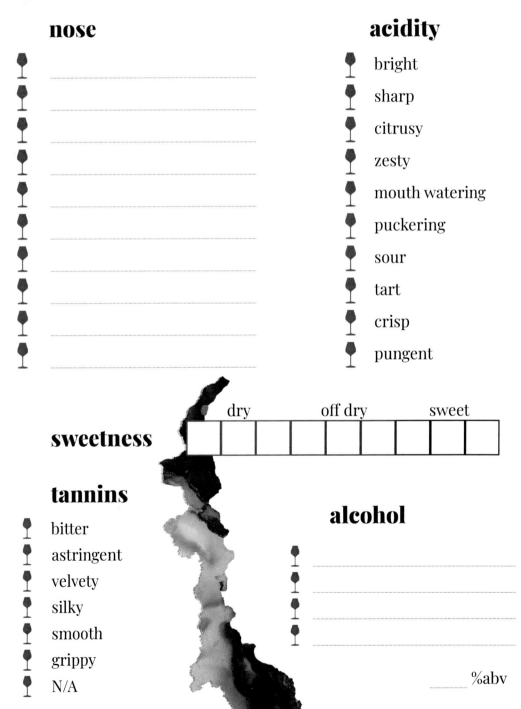

acidity

- bright
- sharp
- citrusy
- zesty
- mouth watering
- puckering
- sour
- tart
- crisp
- pungent

sweetness

dry				off dry			sweet	

tannins

- bitter
- astringent
- velvety
- silky
- smooth
- grippy
- N/A

alcohol

.... %abv

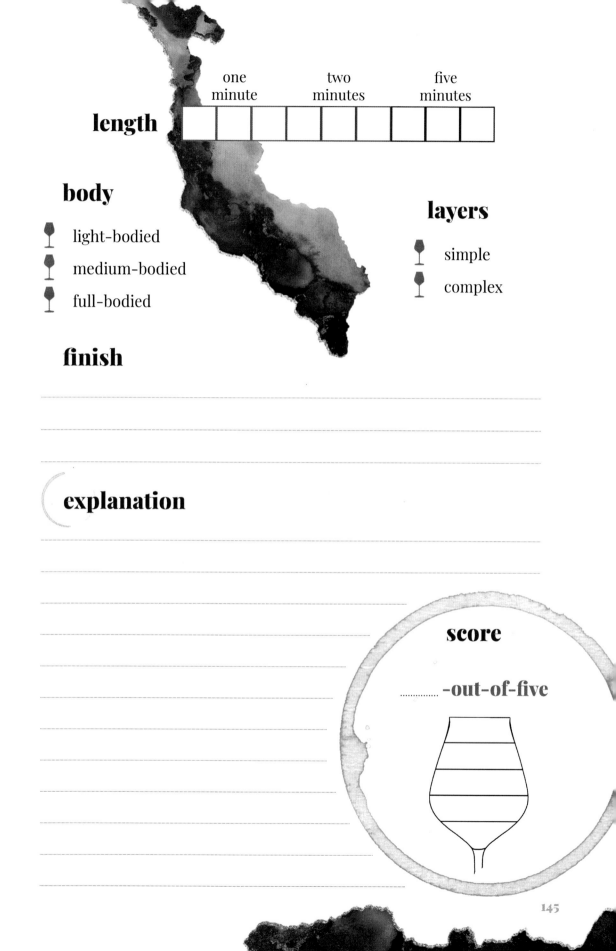

length

one minute		two minutes			five minutes			

body

light-bodied

medium-bodied

full-bodied

layers

simple

complex

finish

explanation

score

............-out-of-five

Name of Wine		Region	
Vintage of Wine		Country	
Grape Varietal		Price	
Place of Purchase		Date of Scoring	

nose

acidity

bright

sharp

citrusy

zesty

mouth watering

puckering

sour

tart

crisp

pungent

sweetness

dry   off dry   sweet

tannins

bitter

astringent

velvety

silky

smooth

grippy

N/A

alcohol

_____ %abv

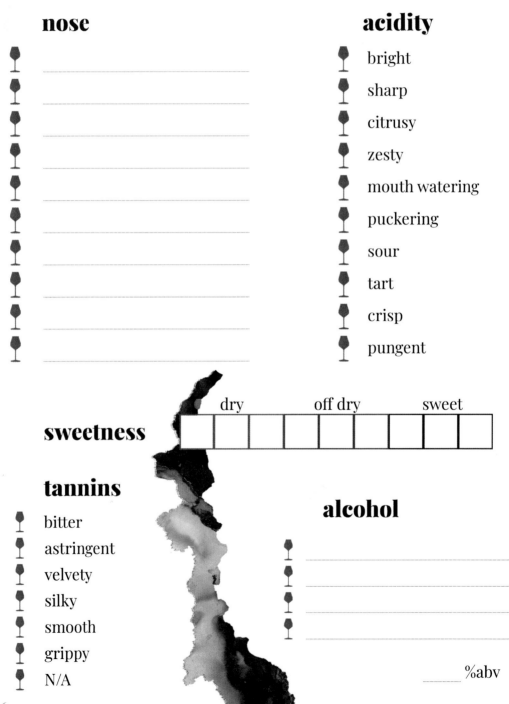

length

one minute   two minutes   five minutes

body

light-bodied

medium-bodied

full-bodied

layers

simple

complex

finish

explanation

score

............-out-of-five

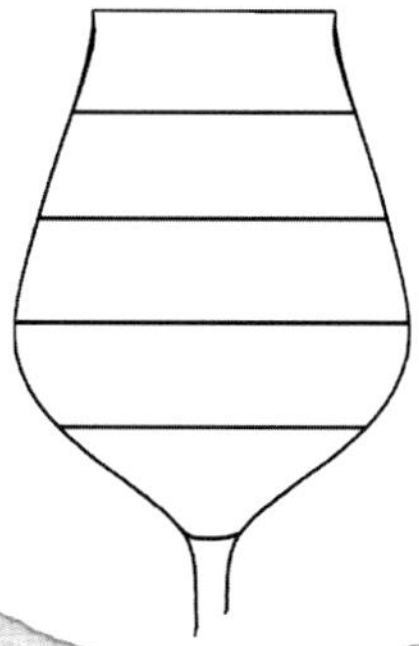

Name of Wine	....	Region	....
Vintage of Wine	....	Country	....
Grape Varietal	....	Price	....
Place of Purchase	....	Date of Scoring	....

nose

acidity

bright

sharp

citrusy

zesty

mouth watering

puckering

sour

tart

crisp

pungent

sweetness

dry				off dry			sweet	

tannins

bitter

astringent

velvety

silky

smooth

grippy

N/A

alcohol

.... %abv

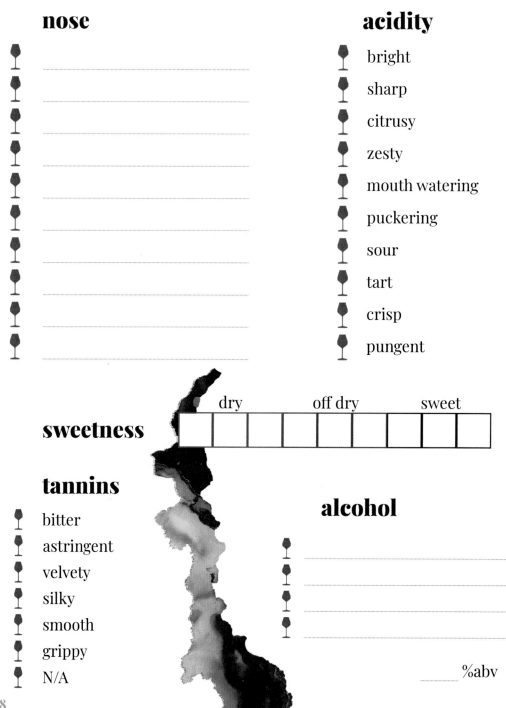

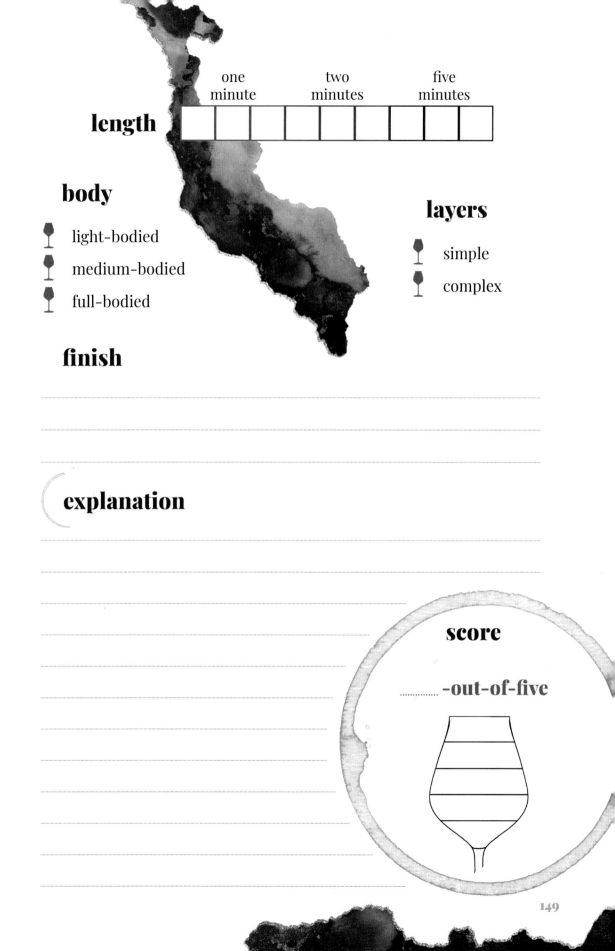

length

one minute			two minutes			five minutes		

body

🍷 light-bodied

🍷 medium-bodied

🍷 full-bodied

layers

🍷 simple

🍷 complex

finish

explanation

score

.... -out-of-five

149

Name of Wine		Region	
Vintage of Wine		Country	
Grape Varietal		Price	
Place of Purchase		Date of Scoring	

nose

acidity

bright

sharp

citrusy

zesty

mouth watering

puckering

sour

tart

crisp

pungent

sweetness

dry				off dry			sweet	

tannins

bitter

astringent

velvety

silky

smooth

grippy

N/A

alcohol

%abv

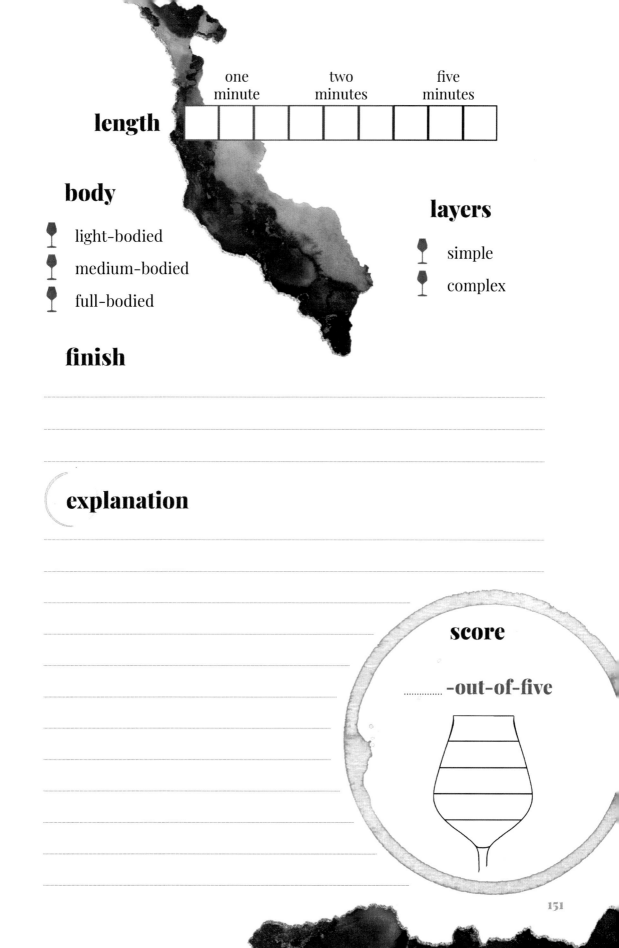

length

one minute			two minutes			five minutes		

body

🍷 light-bodied

🍷 medium-bodied

🍷 full-bodied

layers

🍷 simple

🍷 complex

finish

....

....

explanation

....

....

....

....

....

....

....

....

....

....

score

.... -out-of-five

Name of Wine		Region	
Vintage of Wine		Country	
Grape Varietal		Price	
Place of Purchase		Date of Scoring	

nose

acidity

- bright
- sharp
- citrusy
- zesty
- mouth watering
- puckering
- sour
- tart
- crisp
- pungent

sweetness

			dry			off dry			sweet		

tannins

- bitter
- astringent
- velvety
- silky
- smooth
- grippy
- N/A

alcohol

_____ %abv

length

body

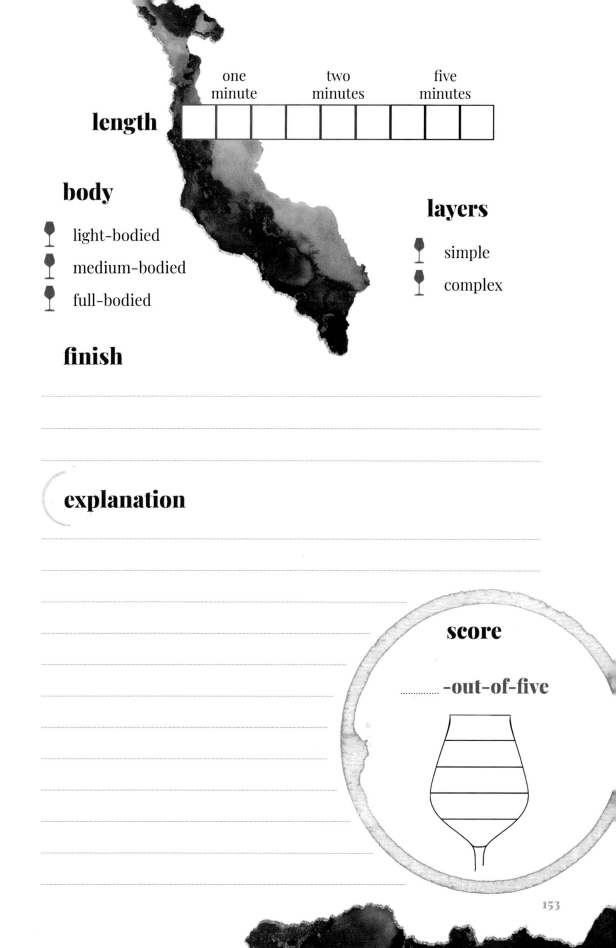

- light-bodied
- medium-bodied
- full-bodied

layers

- simple
- complex

finish

explanation

score

.... -out-of-five

Name of Wine		Region	
Vintage of Wine		Country	
Grape Varietal		Price	
Place of Purchase		Date of Scoring	

nose

acidity

bright

sharp

citrusy

zesty

mouth watering

puckering

sour

tart

crisp

pungent

sweetness

dry				off dry			sweet	

tannins

bitter

astringent

velvety

silky

smooth

grippy

N/A

alcohol

_____ %abv

length

one
minute

two
minutes

five
minutes

body

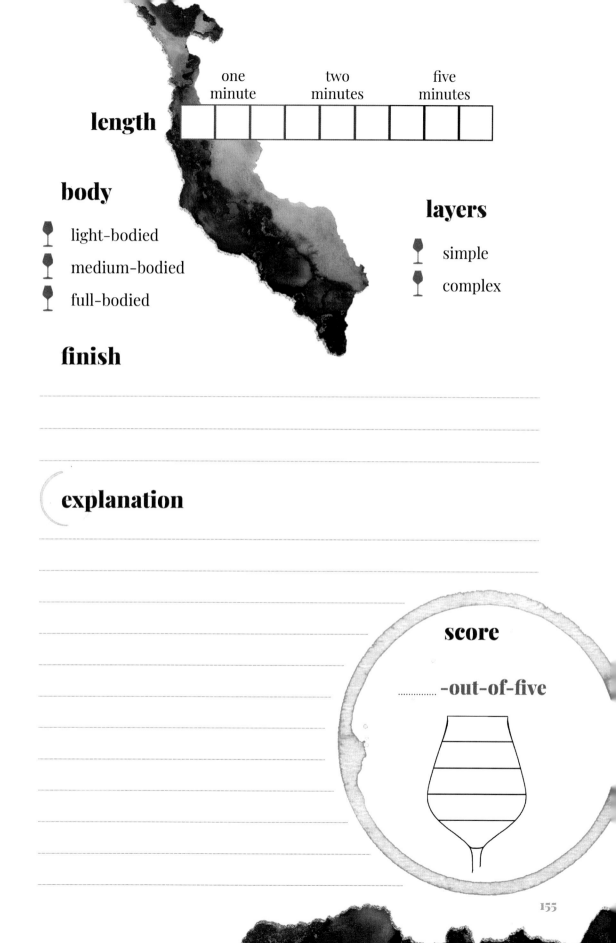

light-bodied

medium-bodied

full-bodied

layers

simple

complex

finish

....

....

....

explanation

....

....

....

....

score

.... -out-of-five

....

....

....

....

....

Name of Wine		Region	
Vintage of Wine		Country	
Grape Varietal		Price	
Place of Purchase		Date of Scoring	

nose

acidity

- bright
- sharp
- citrusy
- zesty
- mouth watering
- puckering
- sour
- tart
- crisp
- pungent

sweetness

			dry		off dry		sweet		

tannins

- bitter
- astringent
- velvety
- silky
- smooth
- grippy
- N/A

alcohol

_____ %abv

length

one minute   two minutes   five minutes

body

🍷 light-bodied

🍷 medium-bodied

🍷 full-bodied

layers

🍷 simple

🍷 complex

finish

....

....

....

explanation

....

....

....

....

....

....

....

....

....

....

score

.... -out-of-five

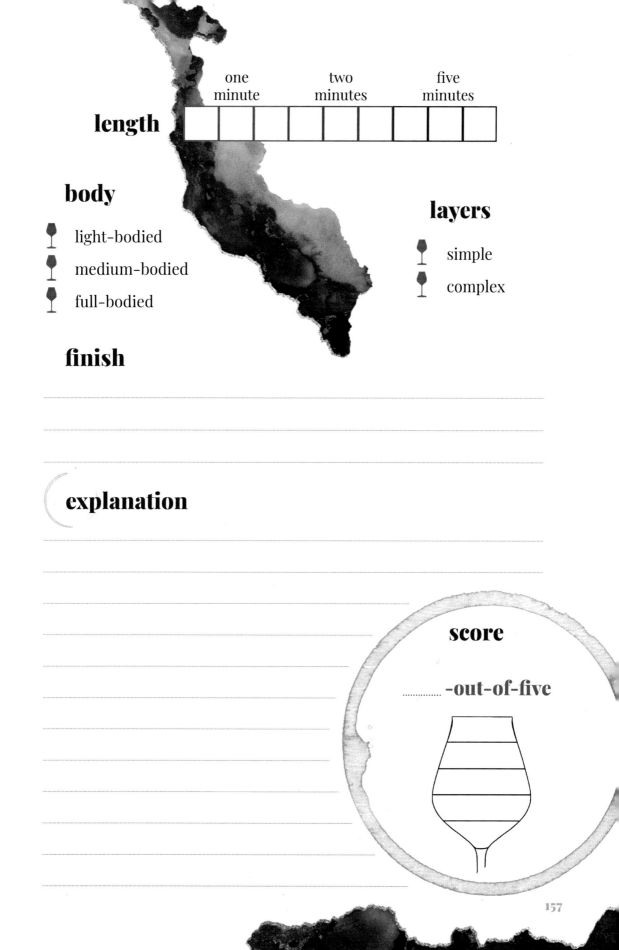

157

Name of Wine	....	Region	....
Vintage of Wine	....	Country	....
Grape Varietal	....	Price	....
Place of Purchase	....	Date of Scoring	....

nose

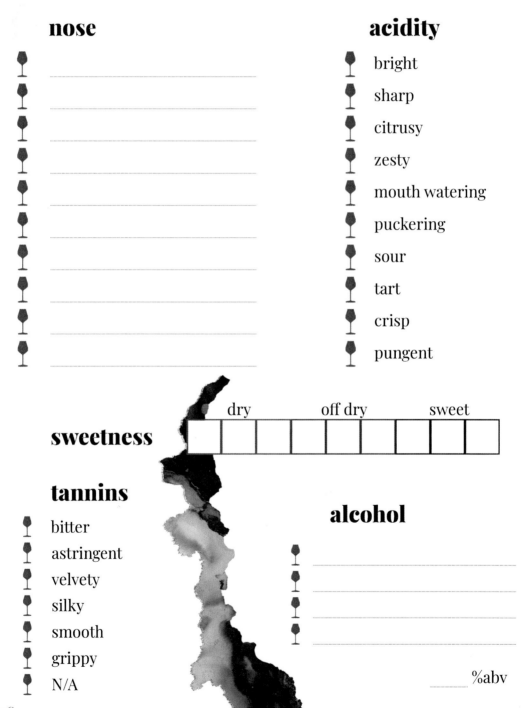

acidity

- bright
- sharp
- citrusy
- zesty
- mouth watering
- puckering
- sour
- tart
- crisp
- pungent

sweetness

			dry			off dry			sweet	

tannins

- bitter
- astringent
- velvety
- silky
- smooth
- grippy
- N/A

alcohol

_____ %abv

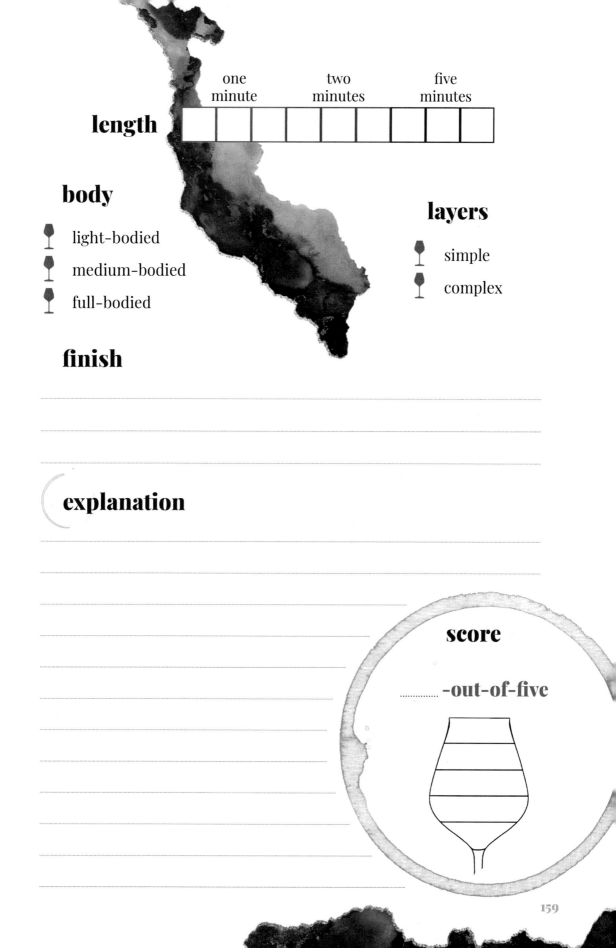

length

	one minute			two minutes			five minutes	

body

🍷 light-bodied

🍷 medium-bodied

🍷 full-bodied

layers

🍷 simple

🍷 complex

finish

explanation

score

.... -out-of-five

Name of Wine		Region	
Vintage of Wine		Country	
Grape Varietal		Price	
Place of Purchase		Date of Scoring	

nose

acidity

- bright
- sharp
- citrusy
- zesty
- mouth watering
- puckering
- sour
- tart
- crisp
- pungent

sweetness

dry			off dry			sweet		

tannins

- bitter
- astringent
- velvety
- silky
- smooth
- grippy
- N/A

alcohol

_____ %abv

length

one minute			two minutes			five minutes		

body

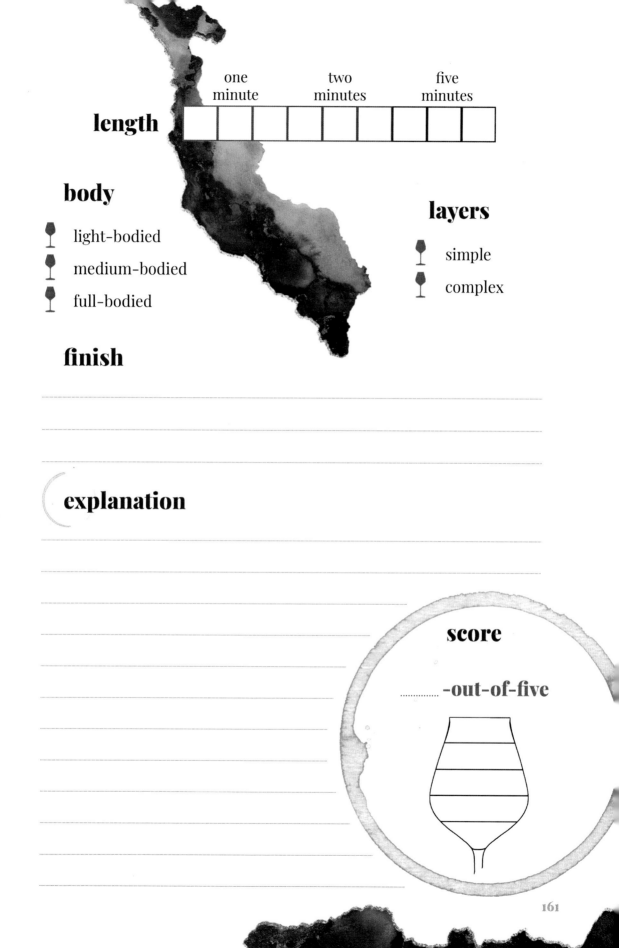

 light-bodied

 medium-bodied

 full-bodied

layers

 simple

 complex

finish

explanation

score

.... -out-of-five

Name of Wine		Region	
Vintage of Wine		Country	
Grape Varietal		Price	
Place of Purchase		Date of Scoring	

nose

acidity

- bright
- sharp
- citrusy
- zesty
- mouth watering
- puckering
- sour
- tart
- crisp
- pungent

sweetness

	dry			off dry			sweet	

tannins

- bitter
- astringent
- velvety
- silky
- smooth
- grippy
- N/A

alcohol

_____ %abv

length

one minute			two minutes			five minutes		

body

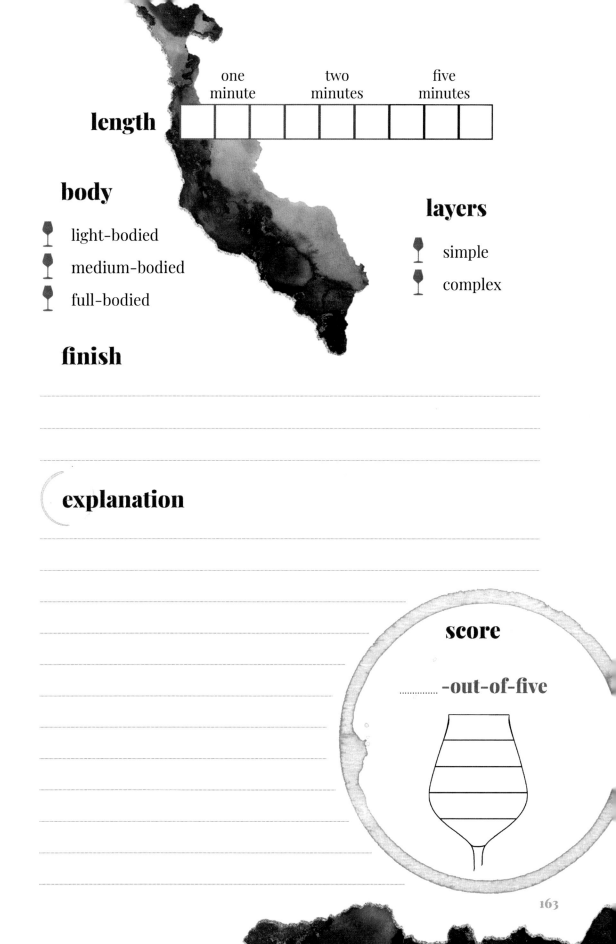 light-bodied

medium-bodied

full-bodied

layers

simple

complex

finish

....

....

....

explanation

....

....

....

....

....

score

.... -out-of-five

....

....

....

Name of Wine		Region	
Vintage of Wine		Country	
Grape Varietal		Price	
Place of Purchase		Date of Scoring	

nose

acidity

- bright
- sharp
- citrusy
- zesty
- mouth watering
- puckering
- sour
- tart
- crisp
- pungent

sweetness

dry				off dry			sweet	

tannins

- bitter
- astringent
- velvety
- silky
- smooth
- grippy
- N/A

alcohol

_____ %abv

length

one minute			two minutes			five minutes		

body

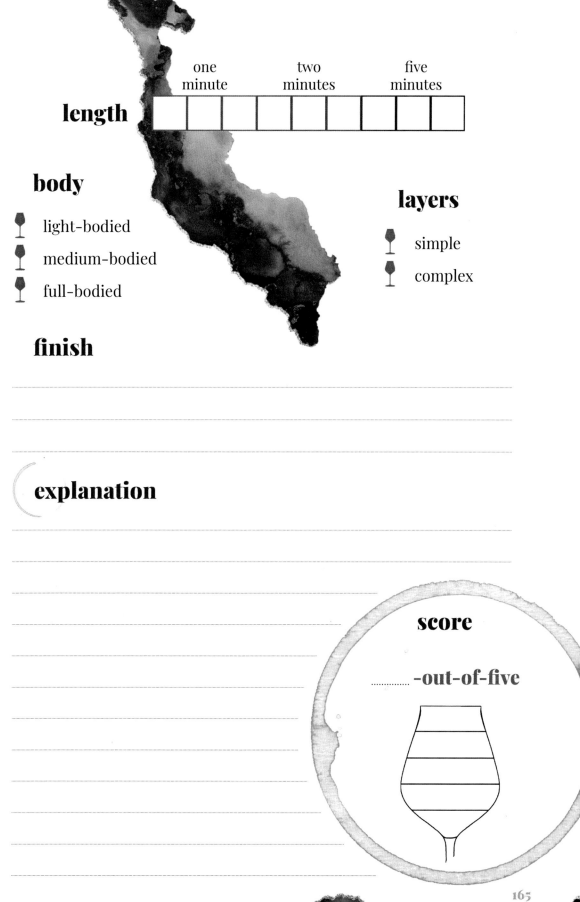

light-bodied

medium-bodied

full-bodied

layers

simple

complex

finish

explanation

score

............-out-of-five